My Second-Hand Cats

Audrey Nash

authorHOUSE®

AuthorHouse™ UK Ltd.
500 Avebury Boulevard
Central Milton Keynes, MK9 2BE
www.authorhouse.co.uk
Phone: 08001974150

First published by AuthorHouse 10/31/2008

ISBN: 978-1-4389-1400-8 (sc)

Printed in the United States of America
Bloomington, Indiana

This book is printed on acid-free paper.

Contents

In memory
of my one adorable niece,
Vanessa Ridge,
who loved cats (and dogs),

but was so wonderful with people.

Introduction

Of the thirteen cats I have owned or still own, only one came to me in his kitten days. Two of the others were under a year old when I first had them, but one was well into his sixteenth year. So it is this fact which gives the book its title. Older cats can settle into new surroundings very well indeed if one takes just a little care to give them time to adjust.

Peter and I married later on in life than most couples and we did not produce a family. That has left me open to the remark from one or two people, "You have no children, so your cats must be like children". Perish the thought! Cats are animals and it is unkind to treat them as anything else. To treat pets as people in fur coats is a sign that all is not well with the person who acts in this way. I once heard someone say, "My dog is the child I never had." No, being kind to an animal starts with accepting it for what it is, not making it into a substitute for something else.

Six of the feline characters in this book were still with us at the time the book was written in 2006.

Sooty, the little black cat of the penultimate chapter, has made a bid to be regarded as co-author of this slim volume. At least she has sat on my lap each time I have worked at it. Realistically her main

contribution to the writing has been sometimes nuzzling my fingers as I type and also shedding black hairs over the computer keyboard. If she rests her head on my thumbs, she enjoys having her chin tickled while I type. But she has provided the subject matter for one chapter of this story.

You could read this book as a kind of warning. After all, once upon a time, in fact a quarter of a century ago, we were a respectable one-cat household. Then cats began to happen to us in ways that you can read about here. You will notice that the last chapter is entitled, 'Six Cats in One Garden'! That is our current situation. This book charts our progress down that slippery slope!

However, what I hope is that in the following pages I can share with you something of the delight that these cats, all such different characters, have brought me.

Smokey helping me in the Stoneleigh garden

Chapter 1: Smokey, My First Cat

My earliest memories include animals. I had that enormous privilege of being brought up in the country during the middle of the last century. Yes, there was a war, and in a Suffolk village surrounded by aerodromes one could hardly ignore that, and yet it impinged on my early life very little. To a young child's perception how things are is regarded as what is normal. American soldiers, white and coloured, war planes and army vehicles were all seen around the area frequently and I accepted all this as if it were the usual state of affairs.

Father had a poultry farm, or as I was proud to tell, an accredited breeding poultry farm, which meant that the majority of fertile eggs were sent to the hatchery and so became chickens rather than omelettes. The birds were the glossy red brown Rhode Island Reds or Light Sussex, white with black feathers in tail and wings. There were also a few beautiful, if somewhat batty, Leghorn cockerels to produce

cross bred chicks at the hatchery. As I often helped close up the chicken huts at dusk to ensure that all were safe for the night, I met many a hedgehog and developed a real affection for these delightful little animals.

The other side of my father's business was a nursery garden, selling trees, shrubs and hardy plants. Plants were very much his first love. He would talk plants morning, noon and night. He did not advertise at all. The business grew through word of mouth recommendation. Customers could see how the plants they might wish to buy actually grew in father's own private garden. There, however, they would also see all sorts of horticultural treasures which he did not propagate for sale. No wonder gardening was to become my main hobby later on.

For much of the year milk came from our two goats, Wendy and White Beauty. The latter was a Saanen, a pleasant enough animal, but not really living up to her name. Wendy was a Toggenburg. It was often my job to milk them both at weekends and holidays. I vividly remember milking Wendy, who was very much a creature with a mind of her own. My allocation of just two hands simply was not adequate. My problem was that I had to hold one of Wendy's hind legs with one hand to persuade her to stand something like still and milk her with the other one. That left no further hands either to steady the jug which received the milk or to prevent her from chewing my hair which she did quite regularly. But she was a splendid milker.

The other official animals on the place were the two cats, Tommy, a black one, and Tibby, a handsome black and white. Both were big neutered toms and formidable hunters and yet sweet natured to handle. So I grew up with a couple of very tolerant cats. So tolerant were they that I remember dressing them up in dolls' clothes. On one occasion they took alarm at something and Tommy, or was it Tibby, ran off tripping over his night-dress! He soon let me catch him again and relieve him of it.

Cat care in those days was very basic. About the only time in their lives when the cats would see a vet was when they were neutered. For their first year they were fed on bread and milk and cooked lites, offal that is unlikely to be on sale at all nowadays. After that they simply had a bowl of bread and milk each day and were expected to be able to catch the rest of their food. This they succeeded in doing as mice, field voles, rats and rabbits were abundant. Did the cats of those days have stronger digestive systems? I never remember any time when the ever available milk upset their tums as it would do nowadays with many of our pet cats.

Tibby and Tommy lived into their teens. They were followed by cats who came and went all too quickly. One who made quite an impression was a very big tabby, Tinker. He would see off the neighbour's dog if it dared to set foot on his patch.

Meanwhile I moved on from school to Royal Holloway College, then part of London University. Reading English there was followed up by the one year post-graduate teacher training course at Maria Grey College in London. For these years my life was mainly catless: in fact I had very little contact with animals.

I do remember that during this one year course I slept on the ground floor of the college with my window open. One night at three in the morning I was awakened by something landing on my bed. My first thought was that it must be the cat belonging to one of our lecturers. Puss lived at the college with her during term time, but I had never yet seen her. Yes, the night-time intruder was this cat. She paid me several welcome night visits in succeeding weeks. Puss was off-white due to London grime. Apparently she became pure white during vacations, which she spent with her owner somewhere in the country, .

Then there was Wimboo. By that time I was teaching at the new secondary modern school about three miles from my parents' home. A teacher was going to get rid of this kitten if no one wanted it and I persuaded my parents, who were currently without a cat, to take it on. So it was delivered to me at school first thing in the morning. I put the kitten, with all needed facilities, in my stock cupboard, which was like a very small room. It would stay there just for the morning, as my parents would collect it at mid-day on their way home from shopping.

Every time I looked in the cupboard to check on its welfare it was snoozing on the biography of William Booth, hence its somewhat unusual name.

My parents had Wimboo for a long time, but I only saw him on my visits to them as I moved away from Suffolk again soon after this. Later they took on a Siamese kitten and Wimboo became unsociable, often refusing to eat. This went on for a few months and then my parents took Wimboo to the vet. He was given a thorough once over and the conclusion was that jealousy was the cause of his problems. He improved slowly with the passage of time.

Over the next dozen years or so I enjoyed animals when I met them, but that was not very often. My accommodation was not conducive to having my own pets. After a total of nine years' teaching I took two years out, back at college to complete a degree in theology. Then I returned to teaching with a job in Stockwell. My, that was an eye-opener! I was only glad that it was my tenth year teaching and not my first.

It only lasted one year, I made sure of that. I knew well in advance that I had got a job as head or the religious education department at a school in Tonbridge for the following academic year. I decided that I would look around for a year to get an idea of properties, then I would buy a house. I was a bit tired of the various places: digs, rooms, flats, where teachers can be kept when not otherwise required!

I had been living first in just a bed-sit and then a flat in Oakleigh Park. I often spent time with friends, mother and daughter, from the little church I belonged to in nearby New Barnet. One day I noticed a beautiful tom cat, real blue grey with white paws and white shirt and a very distinct little black nose leather, coming onto their kitchen window sill. He was a stray who kept coming to them and now they were feeding him. But they did not really want to keep him. I said that I would like to have him when I had my own house.

That happened sooner than I was expecting. Early on in my first year in Tonbridge I began to look round a few houses to get the idea of what was available and what I could afford. But with the sixth one I saw I had that strong sense, "This is it!"

There was a good enough way to test that out. I had not had time to save up all the necessary deposit after having taken two years out of teaching to read theology at college. My father had said something about a loan. I calculated that I needed an extra five hundred pounds. So I prayed that if this house was the right one, when I reminded Father about the loan he would name five hundred pounds as the amount offered.

I phoned my parents and asked my father rather cautiously, "What could you let me have without inconvenience to yourself?"

The reply came back "Five hundred pounds!"

Within two months that house was mine and I settled down to repaying both my father's loan and the mortgage.

It was not long before I asked about the grey cat. Yes, he was still available, so we fixed a day for my friends to bring him over. Unfortunately the cat was not consulted in these arrangements, which required them all to set out around 10 a.m.. Puss did not appear until 4 p.m. and then they had the journey from Barnet to Tonbridge. Our leisurely day together did not quite work.

So for the first time ever I had my very own cat, Smokey. It felt strange to be responsible for something alive! Smokey did not seem to know too much about how to behave in a house, though he did get the idea of normal feline toilet training after about the first week and a few disasters. Also I let him out far too soon for a cat in a totally new area. He was gone for a whole fourteen hours. But thankfully he did come back and gradually we got to know each other.

Now that I had my own house I also had my very first garden. Plants for this arrived from my father's nursery well packed in dry straw in a large wicker hamper. That would make a fine bed for Smokey in the garage! This was otherwise redundant as I had no car. I did not take up driving till much later on.

At first I left the garage door open for Smokey and a friend agreed to come and cut out a cat entrance in it. Only when the friend arrived did we notice that in fact the garage windows opened easily and would give Smokey good access. He seemed happy enough with these arrangements.

I began to suspect that he was an entire tom and that this was the reason he had become a stray. So I was contemplating taking him to the vet, when I happened to call on a neighbour. She had an entire tom who had free access to her house. One good smell of that house and Smokey's appointment with the vet was not longer delayed, I can assure you!

He settled down to being a lovely affectionate pet cat, enjoying attention and a lap and coming readily to a call. Generally I only allowed him in the house when I was home and up and he had the option of his well used bed in the garage for the rest of the time. A kind neighbour readily fed him whenever I went away for a few days.

Sometime in the winter I noticed that Smokey was coughing so I phoned the vet. Smokey had cat flu. He was desperately ill. Great pussy tears rolled down his nose. I kept him indoors, just taking him down the garden now and then to see if he wanted outdoor facilities and then bringing him back indoors straight away. How he pulled through I do not know, as for at least three days he did not eat or drink and I knew nothing then of the importance of getting fluid into him. But he not only survived; as far as I could discern, he made a complete recovery.

I was well settled at Tonbridge. I had a good job and my house was only about five or so minutes' walk from my school, yet not in a position where I was always tripping over pupils out of hours. I had joined what became Tonbridge United Reformed Church and was extremely happy in the fellowship of the friendly people there. I also had a really lovely pet cat. So I was not expecting much to change when I went away on holiday in the summer of 1973.

Margaret, who was in charge of music at school, was a good friend and this was the second time we had holidayed together in the Lake District. During that week at the Pillar Hotel in the Langdales, Margaret would often go back to her room after supper, but I stayed in the lounge with most of the other guests. One of these was Peter, a single Baptist minister. We chatted together most evenings.

Come the last day, Margaret was going off to Kendal to visit friends, and Peter asked me to go for a walk. What a walk it was! We went over the Crinkles and Bowfell and down Rossett Gill. We shared our stories of how we had come to a living faith in Jesus Christ. We chatted about all sorts of other things too, but as we came to the the bottom of the Langdale Valley and were walking back towards the car, we fell into a long silence. Then Peter asked if he could visit me when his holiday, which was to last for a further two weeks, was over.

When Peter came to visit me, and sat close to me, Smokey's jealousy was visible. Who was this interloper with whom he must share me? At first I rather felt that Peter and Smokey glared at each other from different parts of the room, each resenting the presence of the other! However, Peter quickly accepted that it was "Love me, love my cat!" and anyway, he liked cats. So he made an effort to get to know Smokey. Smokey came round eventually. Peter and I married in July 1974.

We married because we loved each other and wanted to share our lives together. We decided that we would do this better if I left teaching and supported Peter and shared in his work: after all, much of my training and experience would help with this. Thus in spite of the demands of Peter's work, we have never been short of time together. This has been one of the reasons why in our marriage we have developed a deep friendship and easy companionship.

So Smokey and I left Tonbridge. My neighbour had fed him during our honeymoon and then we drove over to collect him, having carefully arranged completion of sale on my house so that Smokey could stay there until we could do this. He settled in with us in the chalet bungalow in Stoneleigh, near Epsom, which had become the new manse of the Stoneleigh Baptist Church, where Peter was the minister.

Here Smokey had his own cat flap so he could please himself where he spent his nights. He was the first and last of my cats to have that choice! None of the others, with the exception of the only kitten among them, was used to nights in before coming to me, but each adjusted with no apparent problems. Of course, they always have drinking water and litter trays to see them through the nights, though most regard a litter tray as being for emergencies only.

Smokey enjoyed having me around so much more. He frequently came with me when I went out in the garden. On several occasions, as I stooped or knelt down to do some weeding or planting, he jumped on my back: he was never far away from me.

Another advantage for Smokey was that here we were in a less densely catted area, so he was not having ongoing problems about his territory. He had far too many fights in Tonbridge.

One day as Smokey was settling down indoors for the evening he had either a stroke or a heart attack. For a while he was totally disorientated and tended to walk round in circles restlessly. In time this improved, but he never wholly recovered. His sense of smell was so badly affected that he needed strong smelling food to tempt him to eat. But he could get around our garden and did not seem to be in any distress. About a year later a further seizure left him in a worse condition and the only way forward was to have him put to sleep. He had been with me for about six or seven years and had been of unknown mature years when we first met.

Tinkerbell enjoying her stay in Suffolk

Chapter 2: Tinkerbell, my Best Pussy

After having Smokey it felt so strange to be without a cat. I firmly believe that the best memorial to a good pet cat is the next cat. Only one must reckon on it being a quite different character as cats are so very individual. I was unwise enough to decide that the next cat must also be grey and white. To choose a cat on the basis of its colour really makes no sense, but we were very happy with the result this next time round. When we got the new puss she certainly was a different character from dear old Smokey. But we were soon delighted with her.

A young grey and white cat, about nine months old, was advertised in our local paper and, following my enquiry she was delivered to us at around 9 a.m. one morning for us to have her 'on appro' for the day. The previous owner, who had taken on a few extra cats in need, had

decided she must reduce numbers to seven and this grey and white was one of the surplus. But the owner would call at the end of the day to see how we got on. We got on very well indeed, so the little grey and white cat stayed.

I opened the cat carrier and the contents fled across our living room and up the window. No, not up the curtain: she climbed to the top of our patio door up the little ledges of the numerous window panes. So the first time I held her I was up steps lifting her from almost ceiling height!

Fortunately things improved after that. Tinkerbell, as I called her, spent her 'on appro' day alternating between sitting on my lap and enjoying a fuss, then remembering she was in a strange place and reacting to that by disappearing under the sideboard. She was a pretty enough little cat with an elegant dark grey coat and white on her dainty little oval paws and also on her tummy and chest, with a tiny little patch of white intruding onto her upper jaw. She had quite long legs and a small head. She had a rather squeaky miaow, which she was happy to use very frequently.

By now I had realised that a new cat cannot be let outside until it has had plenty of time to get to know the house as its core territory. But I did make the mistake during that first week of taking Tinkerbell out into the garden on some kind of little harness. However, cooing neighbours could not be persuaded to stop cooing with the result that

Tinkerbell took fright, slipped the harness and made a dash for it. Only a timely grab at her tail stopped her disappearing I do not know where. So that was an experiment not to be repeated.

Two incidents happened in those very early days which I well remember. I had left some raspberry jelly to set rather too near the edge of the sideboard and Tinkerbell jumped onto the sideboard and shot it all over both herself and the floor. So we had a raspberry flavoured puss about the place until she had the chance to clean herself up. Then there was the occasion when Peter put some of his classical music on the record player. Tinkerbell took one look at the source of this sound and fled the room! Clearly she had other tastes.

In the days ahead she learnt that the sound of classical music meant a relaxed Peter. Wherever she was when she heard this, even if she was on my lap, she would go over to Peter, jump on his lap, butt his chin with her head and roll over onto her back in the crook of his arm and expect him to rub her tummy. When she had had enough she would get off and maybe come back to me. No-one could give her a tummy rub to her satisfaction except Peter. Sometimes she would go into his study and demand a cuddle. Peter has prepared several sermons, jotting down his notes and ideas with his right hand and cradling Tinkerbell in the crook of his left arm!

Tinkerbell proved to be a delightful pet who spent much time either on our laps or padding round the garden with me. She seemed to love human company and thrived on the fact that we were so available for her.

Quite early on she began to have bouts of lameness when a swelling would occur just above her right front paw and this obviously caused her a certain amount of discomfort. Visits to the vet resulted in temporary relief after antibiotics, but in no time we were back to square one. Eventually the vet operated on her paw and removed an infected growth which he reckoned she could have been born with. There was one more abcess even after that, but mercifully unlike the others this was not a blind abcess and, after it had drained, there was no more trouble on that score.

She did have to have several teeth out on another occasion before she was three years old. When I brought her home I had put all facilities within easy reach for her. What she wanted was fluid. She drank and she drank, milk and then water, milk and then water again, from one dish to the other for around ten minutes. There were no ill effects as she could apparently digest milk then. As she got older she became completely unable to do so. Even a tiny drop would cause her to vomit. I had to learn that giving cats milk is not a very good idea after all.

Sometimes when we went away neighbours would look after Tinkerbell. But quite early on we decided that when we went up to

Suffolk to visit my parents, she would come with us. She squeaked most of the way, but did not seem upset by the travelling. At first I took great care to keep an eye on her as she explored my parents' cottage and later the garden.

After a couple of visits or so, I think Tinkerbell regarded this as her country estate, run for her special benefit. As soon as I let her out of the cat basket she was thoroughly at home. She found a route onto the roof of the cottage and on one occasion we watched as she walked the length of the ridge tiles. When she was let out first thing in the morning she would follow a complicated route onto the roof so she could appear outside our open bedroom window, perched precariously on the guttering. I would haul her inside for her own safely and thus she had achieved her objective.

Tinkerbell would choose the best places for a snooze and my mother's cat, Snoopy, could have what was left. But I do remember Tinkerbell approaching mother's matronly tabby and putting her face in Snoopy's milk saucer. Snoopy landed a reprimanding paw between Tinkerbell's ears, just once.

Somehow I always managed to make sure that Tinkerbell was comfortable for the journey. First thing in the morning before we set off, I would take her down the garden, dig a little hole and show it to her and she would oblige. I have never even tried to pot any other

cat before a journey, though as you will read later, there was one we sometimes potted during his early travels!

Altogether Tinkerbell might have held the pussy record for the number of times she travelled through the Dartford tunnel! But she not only came to Suffolk with us. She came to Devon and to parts of Sussex and to Gloucestershire. We stayed in a self catering cottage in Sidmouth on about three occasions. The owner, who lived next door, was a bit apprehensive about allowing a cat in her well kept holiday cottage and set a few very reasonable conditions for allowing her to come with us. But, after meeting Tinkerbell and seeing how she behaved, she commended her on behaving just as the Manse cat should and we were told she was welcome with us any time.

Tinkerbell would never under any circumstances use her weaponry on humans. One day I had her at the vets with an abcess close to her tail.

"Hold her by the scruff, down like this: cats always bite down," he said as he was about to clean the abcess out. But this was my Tinkerbell and so I did not bother to do as instructed. The vet cleaned out her abcess while Tinkerbell purred in my arms.

"They are not all like that!" he warned.

Then there were the two quite separate occasions when Tinkerbell took the short route out of a small tree she had climbed. Both times

I was standing underneath trying to persuade her to come down. Her response was simply to let go altogether and I caught her in my arms.

"You could get scratched to bits doing that", said a friend who was watching. Yes with almost any other cat, but not this one.

Another of her exploits up trees was two or three gardens away, but visible to us through our window. Tinkerbell was high up a silver birch tree, one of a little group of trees so close together that some of their branches intertwined. Also up the tree were two or three magpies and they were amusing themselves by taunting her and seeking to lure her right out onto the thinner branches, where with their much lighter weight they had the advantage and knew they were totally safe. The performance went on for half an hour or so, but eventually the magpies gave up and Tinkerbell got herself down and came home.

Peter had been at Stoneleigh for several years before we met each other, and after a total of over eleven years there, felt it time for a move. He was appointed to Dorking Baptist Church. So we moved into the Dorking manse. We had marvellous views of Box Hill from the back of the house and could walk up it without going onto the roads at all.

Tinkerbell's time with us at Stoneleigh had passed without her having much contact with other cats. It was a different matter when we moved to Dorking. There was a large odd tempered tabby, Tiger, who had been used to regarding our garden as part of his territory and he certainly was not going to give that up. Tinkerbell was incredibly unbothered by his presence, usually not noticing him until it was too late. Fortunately he did not go in for a prolonged fight, just a bonk to let her know who was boss. If she saw him out of the window, she scarcely reacted.

But there was another local tabby who, when seen at a distance, looked very much like Tiger, but this one had a white end to its tail. On the less frequent occasions when Tinkerbell saw him she would caterwaul, even if he was at a distance where I could only just distinguish his white tail ending. This was strange as he was not aggressive towards her. Tinkerbell's caterwaul was strange too: perhaps she needed some voice training or more practice, but it was one of the oddest sounds I have heard from a cat.

Both manse and garden at Dorking were larger than at Stoneleigh and Tinkerbell seldom wandered off the premises. With a bigger garden for me to enjoy, she had plenty to do pottering around with me.

Spud and Sparkle on the kitchen worktop

Chapter 3: A Home for Spud

One evening we received a phone call from Vanessa, my niece, who was living in London at the time and working at Queen Elizabeth College. A call from Vanessa was always welcome: we thought a great deal of her as she was such a delightful and original person. She was concerned for a little cat, Spud by name, in dire need of a home. Spud was constantly crossing busy London roads. She was either getting locked in or out of the college office at weekends and neither option was good. The Suffolk relatives would not have her, Vanessa said, so we were the last resort.

I asked her to hold on while I had a quick discussion with Peter.

"She's never asked us to do anything before. We could say, 'Bring her here, and we'll find a good home for her.'"

So it was agreed that Vanessa and friend, Dave, were to bring Spud to us the next Saturday, that was in two days' time. Only we never did

find a good home for Spud, not in the remaining sixteen years of her life. We gave up looking remarkably quickly.

Spud and Vanessa and Dave arrived some time on Saturday morning. I had already prepared the small bedroom to receive Spud. She was a small black and white cat with a Felix nose, white paws and underparts, though perhaps the white on her nose was over a smaller area than on the Felix cat. She had beautiful great big eyes. But in the corner of one of these I noticed a damaged membrane of her 'third eyelid'. This was the result of a fight, but mercifully no infection had followed.

She came out of her travel basket and immediately showed great interest in her food. Then she purred.

"That's the first time I've heard her purr out loud like that!" Vanessa commented. I was to learn that Spud did indeed use her purr very sparingly.

Vanessa had known Spud since her kitten days when she had belonged to a friend of hers in London. But when her friend sold the flat the cat was left for the next owner, who was prepared to put out some food, but had no time for the friendly little animal. Spud tried her luck at the local pub, but that did not produce regular meals, at least not for stray cats. Then she turned up at Vanessa's office, clearly hungry and homeless. I might add that I soon discovered that she had acquired fleas and a tape worm during her wanderings.

We left her to settle down for the afternoon while Vanessa, Dave and I went for a walk on Box Hill. Peter stayed in to complete some work.

When we got back, he said, 'I have been upstairs, just to see how little Parsnip is getting on!' She got on well.

Later on that day I left Spud's door open and there was a new box of dry cat food nearby on the landing. Peter came upstairs to find that Spud had chewed a hole in the cardboard box and was inserting her paw and arm into it, so that she could extract the goodies. On seeing Peter, she withdrew with a guilty look. She always tended to melt away if she was watched feeding.

Spud was an affectionate little cat and now that there was a lap to sit on, she was prepared to make the most of it. I tackled the fleas, but the evidence of the tape worm was not to be ignored: those nasty 'rice grains' around a cat's behind. I got a pill from the vet, but there were instructions of no food for twelve hours before the pill and none for three hours afterwards. When I went in Spud's room to give her the pill it was as if she was trying to say, "Yes, it's lovely to see you, but what about my breakfast?" However, she did not have to wait too long for that.

Sometime during her first week or two with us we took her to the vet who kept her in for an anaesthetic and did a superbly neat job

removing that bit of dangling third eyelid. Spud quickly gained in both condition and confidence.

I did realise she could not just be let loose with Tinkerbell from the start, though I should have managed the introductions better than I did. The first day we had her, I had let Spud downstairs and she found Tinkerbell's food in the utility room. This did not meet with Tinkerbell's approval. Our attempt that evening to have a cat each on our laps was not a very wise move either. Anyway, during the next week or two Tinkerbell and Spud did meet up several times and neither really fancied the other. Spud proved to be the bolder character of the two and she was usually boss. However, there was plenty of room in both house and garden for both cats.

Spud was three years old when we had her. Vanessa even managed to retrieve her vaccination certificate from the previous owner's ex-flat and this gave her actual date of birth. Of the thirteen cats I have had Spud was the only one concerning whom I have had that information.

Spud did everything with enthusiasm. I remember calling her once when she was out in the garden and there were great puddles on the paths after heavy rain. Spud arrived in a series of enormous leaps and went straight through the middle of the puddles, splashing water in all directions. Sometimes when I called her she would just rush up and

down the large Bramley apple tree at the side of the garden on her way to me. Trees were for climbing!

Her horticultural education was deficient. She knew that cats eat grass, so she was liable to chew any long green leaves, but fortunately she came to no harm. She knew that cats dig toilet holes for themselves, even if, when surrounded by London pavement, this had been impossible for her. But clearly she had not quite worked out the reason for these excavations. I vividly remember Spud industriously digging and then standing with her front feet down the hole and her bottom stuck up on the surface of the ground on more than one occasion. She did get the hang of it eventually.

She was an athletic, adventurous little cat. There were times when she must have thought her name was 'No-Spud!' For if she was climbing up forbidden things in the house, a sharp "No, Spud", would usually halt her progress. But this was not before she had turned round and answered back with a special miaow reserved for these occasions and that sounded very much like "No!"

Perhaps it was before we had Spud that Tinkerbell first developed cystitis. After this first bout, the vet always let me have one dose of medication in reserve as cystitis would always come on at the most inconvenient times like 10 p.m. on Saturday evening. With medication to hand things were a lot easier and Tinkerbell could be relieved of discomfort quite quickly. A bit later on she was also put on a small vitamin C tablet daily. I remembered that she liked sultanas, so each day I concealed the tablet in a sultana and she ate it gladly. A few years later, Spud also developed cystitis, but the vet thought it unlikely one cat had caught it from the other, though it was unusual to have the only two cats in a household suffering from it. Eventually it cleared up for both of them.

At one stage Spud had to have regular pills and getting a pill down Spud was not easy, even if I wrapped her in a towel. Then she suddenly decided pills did not hurt after all. From then on she would take them like a lamb. I remember that if she was curled up, I only had to awaken her and lift her head a bit, open her mouth and pop the pill in. She would not even bother to get up. She never was difficult about pills after that.

Spud was a bad traveller at first. But we decided to try to take her to Devon with us on a self-catering holiday. We used some medication from the vet to calm her down on both journeys, but did not like the result of a somewhat drunk looking cat, who was wobbly on her legs, for the rest of the day and so we decided that this was not to be repeated. Then on one of the very short vet trips Spud behaved perfectly in the car. She had apparently decided that a ride in the car did not hurt either! So by the next time we took her on holiday she had

decided she did not mind cars and travelled without any sign of being upset. She was a good feline traveller from then on.

We stayed a few times in a self-catering bungalow on a working farm not far from Hay Tor in Devon. One day the farmer took his sheep into a big shed to keep their fleeces dry for shearing the next day. Whether the sheep were fed then or not, I do not know: I suspect not. They broke out of the shed, (not difficult judging from its condition,) and surrounded the bungalow, eating everything in sight from rhubarb to azaleas. Spud looked up and saw them. Those big eyes got bigger and bigger. Here we were totally besieged by sheep! I am quite sure that she had never even seen one sheep in her life before this. Her face was a picture. The farmer soon collected his sheep, but I guess nothing in that garden needed trimming for a long time.

Chapter 4: A Stray and Some Visitors

While we were still in Dorking a beautiful white and tabby tom cat turned up in our garden one summer's day. He hung around and seemed in no mind to go away. A little straw placed under a cloche was appreciated as a bed. He did not seem to have anywhere else to go. At first I gave him milk and he got through a great deal of it, but as soon as he was offered food he drank a lot less. I named him Silver.

Silver had a persistent cough. We had him to the vet to be neutered. We adopted him. But the vet was not able to get wholly on top of the cough. However, for a while Silver was not too bad. He quickly settled down as my pet. He was a friendly cat, who liked a lap. Unfortunately he never looked to check whether or not it was already occupied and

both Tinkerbell and Spud had the odd surprise when Silver landed right on top of them.

I was keeping Tinkerbell and Spud separate at nights in those days so as not to overstrain their tolerance of each other. We had five bedrooms in the Dorking manse, so it was not difficult to find another room for Silver at night. One night Vanessa came to stay.

"Bags a room with a cat in it", she said, so she slept in the same room as Silver!

But Silver's cough was worrying and all was not well. Treatment at the vets did not make any progress and this was not helped by different vets being on duty and pursuing different symptoms. Maybe nothing could have been done. Anyway, one day Silver was left at the vets for treatment and he died there that day. He was only a youngish cat and we had him for just three months.

Peter was out that evening on some church business. I believe the best way to get through a bereavement is to be able to express one's grief. The death of a pet is a minor bereavement. So I was prepared to have a good howl and then talk to the Lord about Silver, about my puzzlement, our inability to help him and the waste of such a beautiful young cat. I remember that evening vividly. It is as if I can see now the chair I sat in, looking out of our patio window.

I saw nothing. I heard nothing. Yet in the silence, without speech, the words, "I created him" came to me as distinctly as any words could.

Those three words changed that evening immediately. So God cared about Silver a great deal more than ever I could. Never mind if there were things I could not understand, what did they matter now? Silver had been lent to me to look after. We had done everything we could for him.

Shortly after that we had a week's holiday at home, going out locally for days. I reflected to myself that the week's holiday cost less than we had spent on Silver. I was quite happy about that. One day we went to Arundel and had a good look round.

"I'm glad we took Silver in and did what we could for him", said Peter as we were looking in a shop window. That helped too.

Two other cats made their mark on our time at Dorking. An elderly lady in the church was in very poor health. She had two much loved tabbies and was worried about what to do with them while she went into hospital. I said I would have them in our home as visiting them in her flat to look after them was not really practical as I still was not a car driver in those days.

The larger cat, a really beautiful animal whose tabby markings made a black necklace on his chest, was named Tinkerbell. To avoid confusion I generally referred to him as Big Tinkerbell. The other smaller cat was Tiger. I kept them in the utility room while they were with me for three or four weeks.

I must have still been giving our Tinkerbell some lites in those days. Unwisely as it proved, I gave some to Tiger. Next day he clearly had a problem with his mouth. I opened it and had a look. To my horror I found that a completely circular piece of lites was firmly wedged around his tongue.

Peter was away for a few days and the vet's surgery was at the other end of town. This might be a good walk, but it was too far to carry a cat. I begged a good friend for transport and off to the vets we went. Tiger was left there for the day. He had to have an anaesthetic to remove the offending ring! I was so relieved to get him home safe and well later on in the day. Yes, we were a little out of pocket, but at least I would be able to return Grace's cat to her safe and sound.

About two years later on, after Tiger had been put to sleep at a good old age, Big Tinkerbell came to stay with me again. He was a lovely animal, the perfect feline gentleman and I got very fond of him. Soon after this Grace's health had deteriorated further and she felt she could no longer keep him. He was already fifteen years old.

"Please don't do anything before I see if I can find him a home", I pleaded.

I prayed about his situation and made a shortlist of likely people in church whom I would ask to home him. The first person I approached

lived in a big house with quite extensive grounds out in the country . She already had two cats and a dog.

"Yes, we can take on another cat", was her immediate response.

So at fifteen Big Tinkerbell went to a new home where he continued to be lovingly cared for during the remaining four years of his life. This cat, who had had such a fear of dogs that he would sometimes be sick if he saw one, got so used to the dog that he would sleep in its bed. He was a placid cat really and occasionally his new owner took him the few miles back into Dorking just to visit Grace.

Our time at Dorking drew to its close and we prepared to move to Chichester, where Peter would take up the pastorate of the Baptist Church. The only problem was that the purchase of the bungalow in which we were to live had not even commenced by our moving date. However, a couple in the church offered us the use of their purpose built flat for the time being. It was joined on to their house in Fishbourne, a village on the outskirts of Chichester . So towards the end of September 1984 we moved into this flat.

It was a long and confusing day for Spud and Tinkerbell, who spent most of it in travel baskets in the car, staying there even after we arrived while our stuff was moved in. Later we were able to let them explore the flat. By then I was tired out and lay down on the settee for a bit with Spud's favourite green rug on top of me. She jumped on that and settled down. Spud made it quite clear that she was already at home in her new surroundings! Tinkerbell did not seem to have any difficulty adjusting either.

Over the next few weeks I did let the two cats out a few times, supervising them as closely as I could. Eventually I decided we were too close to a rather fast road and that both would be better kept indoors for the rest of our stay in Fishbourne.

In spite of that, we lost Spud one day, or at least we could not find her. Yet we knew she was in the flat. We searched all the possible places, under the bed, behind furniture, but that did not reveal her hiding place. Eventually we looked down into the tall wicker linen basket. There right at the bottom was Spud, curled up and looking up at us with those big eyes. She certainly did have a habit of changing her sleeping places quite frequently. Over the years we had her I must have spent quite a few hours enthusiastically calling Spud out in the garden, while she was peacefully snoozing somewhere new in the house.

We moved into the bungalow eleven weeks after our arrival in Chichester and both cats were keen to get out of doors, but they had to get to know the bungalow first. Peter put the steps up to go into the loft for something and Spud got there first! She then exercised her considerable skill at evading capture. It took Peter ages to get hold of

her to bring her down again. After that, whenever we use steps or a ladder for the loft, we make sure all pussies were safely out of the way.

Neither Spud nor Tinkerbell were hunters and so I could feed the birds in the winter without endangering them. Of course food must be put where the cats did not have immediate cover to stalk birds, but provided one used a bit of sense, feeding them was not hazardous from that point of view. We had a couple of severe winters after our move to Chichester and I remember one occasion when I counted at least twenty five blackbirds feeding on the bird food provided for them in the snow on our lawn. A good variety of other birds came too and each spring we had a small flock of reed buntings.

During her sixteen years with us Spud caught only one bird, a fledgling blackbird . She dropped it almost immediately unharmed and after I had picked it up, showed no further interest. Off it went! Tinkerbell was a bit more enthusiastic, but I do remember a mother blackbird being able to frighten her away from her newly fledged young. Tinkerbell's greatest ever hunting achievement had been to catch a young rat and leave it on our lawn at Dorking, just the spot where the deacons of the church were due to go out for a group photograph a few minutes later on.

One day Spud came indoors covered with sharp burrs. If she had tried to get them out herself and swallowed any she could have been in trouble. I took them out of her coat one by one till I was sure she was clear of them. Then I went outside into the garden and dug up the offending plant which used this method of dispersing its seed. So my acaena went on the compost heap, not the last plant to do so in the interests of feline welfare.

Tinkerbell was always ready for a lap and a fuss. Spud would have a lap when she chose and she would come up so quietly that sometimes I would find myself stroking a silky ball on my lap with no recollection of when she had arrived there.

During our fourth year in Chichester, Tinkerbell was slowing up imperceptibly in her responses to me. I could not quite pin anything down: there was not enough change in her to cause alarm. But I remember that when I had to go away for a weekend I was uneasy about leaving her to a friend's care. When I returned she was not at the door to greet me as usual, instead she simply sat up on the chair she was occupying in the study.

It was not long after this that I took her to the vets and she was diagnosed with an infection and provided with antibiotics. But her response to these was slow and as soon as she came off them, infection returned. Then the vet suspected that she had contracted feline leukaemia, which acts like feline aids, weakening the immune system.

It soon became clear that the outlook for my Tinkerbell was not good. When I woke during the night, I would go to her. If I lifted the water dish to her, she would drink, but probably not make the effort to get up and go to the water bowl herself. I sat with her for some time most nights for a while.

It became a question of judging how long to let her go on. The vet reckoned she was not yet in pain, and she was eating and drinking. But it was clear that I would have to let her go before she was in any pain. The day came when we took Tinkerbell to the vet to be put to sleep. She was my best pussy.

Those words I had sensed when I was about to talk to God about Silver helped a great deal at that time. 'I created him'. That could apply not only to Silver. I had had warning that Tinkerbell must go soon, and had partly grieved for her before this. But I just felt so heavy and could hardly get myself moving to do anything. We were about to have a special weekend at church and we were entertaining the guest speaker, Mary. I found it such an effort to get ready.

Peter, who had fetched Mary from the station, had had a word with her in the car! I got a welcoming cup of tea and as we sipped tea, Mary questioned me about Tinkerbell, getting the full story of recent days, encouraging me to talk about her. She had not been the wife of a good pastor for nothing! As I moved into the kitchen to prepare a meal I felt

the weight of heaviness begin to lift, continue to lift, and I was able to cope with the demands of the next few days.

Chapter 5: Sparkle by Name and Nature

As I have already said I believe that the best memorial to a much loved cat is the next cat, even when that puss was as special as Tinkerbell was to us. Spud was not likely to be easy to please, so we were advised that she would probably tolerate a kitten better than another adult.

For the first time we thought of going to a rescue centre to find our next cat. Close to where we lived there was an RSPCA centre and although it was November they did have one litter of kittens ready to home. Out of the three kittens we were shown we chose a little mackerel tabby with white on his paws and chest. He seemed to have the most enormous ears. We named him Sparkle, a name which proved eminently suitable.

Unfortunately he was not as 'ready to home' as we had been led to believe and he had not been properly weaned. He had an upset tummy from the moment we had him. So on our arrival home we had to clean up his travel basket! The next victim was our settee. Further he had not been trained to a toilet tray and we had to watch him like a hawk for a few days until he got the hang of it. He seemed to think the washing machine would make the ideal cat loo and we just managed to prevent him from testing this theory!

So his first few days with us were a bit of a trial for both sides! The vet was concerned about his diarrhoea with its consequent fluid loss and so were we. Sparkle was not keen on the recommended rice and egg diet. Somehow we muddled through those first few days and soon he was eating well, and showing just how lively a fit young kitten can be.

Spud was not favourably impressed by our choice. That is putting it very mildly. She was horrified to see this little tabby thing bouncing round the place and would have nothing to do with it. She would neither eat or drink while it was around, although she did not do too badly on those activities at night when she was on her own. I kept the cat flap firmly locked for about nine days in case she packed her bags and took off.

After a few days someone gave us a ping pong ball. Spud must have fancied herself at feline football, as she found the prospect of a game something she could not resist. So she ended up joining Sparkle after the ball. To our great relief that broke the ice. Eventually we felt we could begin letting Spud out again. Sparkle, of course, could not go out until he was much older.

Sparkle amused himself indoors. He quickly became quite attached to me, often literally so!. He fancied the view of the world from my shoulder. So he would climb up my legs. I was glad when he realised that to get to his chosen perch he must go up the outside of my skirt rather than the inside!. Until he did, I was for ever removing a prickly kitten from my thighs. But after a little he learnt the correct route up to my shoulder and would drape himself round my neck. That year all my Christmas cooking was done with him in that position. If I removed him, he was back in no time, so it was best to accept his arrangement.

The other place it was fun to climb, of course, was up the curtains. Then there was a light mat under which he could disappear. We got used to checking whether there was a bump in it before we stepped on it.

We still went up to Suffolk three times a year to visit my parents. So Sparkle came with us. While he was a kitten there was the small matter of his finding a four hour journey too much for his bladder. Somehow we had worked out a solution before there was any threat of a mishap. I travelled with a cat loo in a dustbin bag tucked under the car seat.

When Sparkle let us know in an unmistakable way that he would like to spend a penny, Peter turned off into a side road as soon as possible and stopped the car. We checked that all the car windows were closed. Then I took the cat loo out of the bag and put it at my feet. We opened Sparkle's travel basket on the back seat. He climbed up the car seat, over my shoulder and down my front to the loo. He sat there for a few minutes with that air of total concentration which only a kitten can muster for such occasions. Then from our front seats we managed to get him back into his basket on the rear seat, saw to it that the basket was securely closed, put the cat loo back in its bag and we were ready to set off again.

Sparkle grew into the most athletic of cats. He was very long limbed. When he ran at speed his hind feet overtook the front ones and this could trip him up if he cornered fast. Sparkle is the only cat I have ever seen lie on the floor and catch his tail over his back. He is also the only one I have seen scratch his ear with the opposite hind leg. For a tom he had a smallish head, with beautiful almond shaped eyes and those large ears. They did seem in proportion when he was fully grown, but while he was a kitten they looked much too big for him. He was a perfectly sweet-tempered cat.

He was so very energetic. Those idyllic days when, although a cat owner I could safely feed the birds on the lawn, were definitely over. As Spud and Sparkle got used to each other, there was a period when he tended to treat her as his soft toy! I do not know what happened, but around the time Sparkle was a year old, we became aware that this situation had changed. Spud had had enough of it. She had put her paw down firmly and thereafter she was to keep Sparkle in his place: she was boss now.

One afternoon Sparkle, who had been outside longer than usual, came through the cat flap into the bungalow and flopped down in the hall way. He seemed stressed. Closer examination showed a grazed leg. Sparkle was reluctant to move. We already had a vets' appointment for Spud in about an hour's time. As I waited for Peter to come home, I thought best to let Sparkle rest where he was. So it was both cats to the vet.

The verdict was the Sparkle had been hit by a car, and that probably his right back thigh had been severely bruised. He was given an injection to help him over the shock and a follow-up appointment was booked. It was soon clear that his bladder was functioning normally, so that was one relief! But by the follow-up visit to the vet he was not making much progress and an X-ray revealed that his femur had cracked right at the top, at his hip joint. The main prescription was cage rest.

Some one kindly lent me a rabbit hutch, where there was just room for Sparkle to lie comfortably and for his food and water and an old oven meat dish as a toilet tray. There he would spend the next few weeks. I could carefully lift him out to have him on my lap, where he would lie quietly. He did not appear restless or fidgety: he just accepted his convalescence. This was so unlike our speedy Sparkle.

After some time he was allowed out of the cage and around the home again, but it was well over three months before he could start exploring the big wide world again. These were to be short outings at first, but at least with Sparkle that was a possibility. I have found that with cats who have continuous access to the house and are kept in at night, their outings are usually fairly brief, even if frequent. When he was fully recovered, Sparkle became the feline athlete again. I do not think he acquired any road sense from his accident.

The next summer Sparkle invented a new game. I was out in the garden near some young fruit trees which were going to crop quite well. Sparkle dashed up an apple tree, swiped his paw at the immature fruit till it fell to the ground, then he jumped down and gave it another pat. Since it would not move any further, he was back up the apple tree for the next one. Our crop was thinned a little before I was able to persuade Sparkle that this was not a very good idea.

After six years at Chichester, Peter and I both felt it was time to move and Peter had given a date for finishing his ministry there. Just at that period there were more Baptist ministers than churches and the latter tended to go for the younger men. There simply were not enough posts to go round, and we ended up with Peter out of work Our accommodation went with the job and so that would disappear too! But God is well able to take care of the material as well as the spiritual side of life. Family money left to us arrived in good time. We had enough to buy a house!

When we were about to move, we went on a three day house hunting trip to Hereford. Any property on a busy road was not worth looking at. The cats must have a sporting chance of their normal life span. So one of the absolute priorities was that the road our house was in must be one which was relatively safe for cats. No road is totally safe, but we could at least do our best.

One other priority was that there would be what I would regard as an adequate garden and that, of course, would be the cats' own core territory. More importantly on that score was the point that gardening was my main relaxation. On the day before we were due to return to Chichester, we saw a suitable property and we both had that feeling, 'This is it!'. We moved into it forty eight days later!

Sparkle found the move a bit traumatic while Spud could be relied on to take life in her stride. We got down to Hereford by car by lunch time with both cats and released them into the empty third bedroom, with necessary feline facilities. I then put a large 'No Entry' notice on

the door. But all the coming and going of a removal was a bit much for our tabby puss.

He was not helped the next day by the gas board's efforts at drilling through our house wall as well as in our drive in order to change the gas pipes. Mercifully on the previous day we had arrived just in time to prevent this from happening on removal's day! But Sparkle found all the noise very unsettling. After a fortnight the cats were let out to explore the garden and they certainly enjoyed climbing the trees.

The back garden was an oblong of grass lawn, with overgrown shrub borders at either side: there was no garden path to the area beyond the ornamental section. At first I was kept well occupied digging the garden and planting the many shrubs, plants and bulbs which I had brought with me, in fact so many that we had had two removals vans: I reckoned I brought about 1000 pots of bulbs and plants with us.

Then Peter used the paving slabs which had been over the front garden to make a path for the back. At first he laid out the slabs on the surface, and viewed them from upstairs as well to see that they were well placed. The new path was to go in a gentle S-shape from the back door to the trellis arch at the end of the ornamental section. To our intense amusement, as soon as the slabs were laid in position, both cats chose to follow the path round, rather than walk in a direct line up the lawn to the house.

Not long after all this Sparkle began fur chewing and had several visits to the vet before he finally gave this up. After a while he happily accepted his new Hereford home. As time went on, he became less lean. At last he had really grown into his ears! He still had a small face for a tom and those beautiful almond shaped eyes. He was a very friendly cat, always pleased to have contact with his humans. Sometimes he would like a lap, especially if I put my feet up on stool: then he could stretch out his full length along my legs.

Sparkle was not bothered by the next three cats who joined us while we still had him, but when we took on a tortie, he could not stand her and did his best to drive her away.

When he was around ten years old I began to notice that Sparkle was losing weight. Further he seemed much slower in his movements. He would go out in the morning as usual, but it would be a long time before he came back up the garden path. Visits to the vet were not very helpful at first as there did not seem to be a clear diagnosis of his problem. His condition was deteriorating and it was very difficult to get him to eat at all. Then someone else at the surgery examined him and suspected a form of cancer. He decided the best way forward was an exploratory operation and if this confirmed his suspicions, then he would not let Sparkle come round. Sparkle did not wake up again as this diagnosis was confirmed.

Black Boy feeling quite at home

Chapter 6: Black Boy

Soon after we had moved to Hereford, I was aware of a black cat coming into the garden quite frequently. He always fled as soon as he saw me. I was watchful least he should regard our garden as his territory and make life difficult for Spud and Sparkle. It just is not feline to welcome newcomers onto your patch with purrs of ecstasy! However, the black cat made little problem about the newcomers. He was more interested in the fact that sometimes I threw kitchen scraps out for the birds. His appearances in our garden were erratically spaced.

But I was concerned one day early the next spring when he came into the garden quite lame and with a visible lump just above one front paw. He still ran away as soon as he saw me, even though using this paw was uncomfortable for him. I pondered what I could do for him. How do you help a cat when you cannot get near to it? Then he disappeared

for a few days. Perhaps he did have owners after all; perhaps he would get the help he needed? But no, he reappeared as lame as ever.

This time I phoned the local Cats' Protection for help. Yes, they would lend me a cat trap. Yes, they would pay to get the black cat neutered and his paw treated. I would have to trap him and get him transported to the vet who dealt with their cases. Afterwards I must release him where I caught him. That after all made good sense, as that was his territory: elsewhere he would feel lost and have to fight the locals to get established.

So I set the cat trap. At first it was frustrating. The black cat went in, but the mechanism worked so slowly that he came out again! Would he risk another go?

After a few days with no further progress I almost gave up trying to catch him. Quite reasonably Cats' Protection were wanting their cat trap back. Then early one morning about the last week in March, I held my breath as the black cat approached the trap again. He went right in, and as he reached towards the food, the trap closed. "First things first" was clearly his motto. He cleared up the food and only when the dish was empty did he begin to show concern about the fact that he was trapped.

I wore gloves to pick up the mesh cage as I had no idea how the cat would react now that he was caught. He did not seem unduly distressed on the journey to the vet. While the cage was on the surgery table the vet tickled him with one finger through the mesh and puss arched his back in response: "I like that!" So although he was so wary of people, he was not a real feral cat, more likely a discarded pet, who had once lived close to his own folk.

He was neutered and deloused as he had lice in his fur. His abcessed paw was cleaned out. I collected him the next day. I was instructed to give him antibiotics for the next few days. Interesting that! It is not always easy to give pills to one's amiable pet cat. How do you give them to one who flees the moment you appear?

The only possibility was to leave food out for him with the medication powdered in it. His visits to our garden were not altogether regular, but he did get most of his antibiotic dose. I kept a very close eye on it, constantly removing the food when Spud and Sparkle were about, but yes, the doctored food did go down the right cat.

Even if the black cat continued to live rough in our garden it was important to be able to handle him in case anything else went wrong and he needed the vet again. Further it was obvious that he had a better chance of keeping well if he was fed properly. So I set about trying to make friends with him.

Food would clearly be my trump card: regular dishes of food even if his visits were still irregular. The first thing was to get him to tolerate my standing close to the house while he ate his food on the lawn at a distance from me. It seemed to take ages before he was happy about this. Gradually I sought to close the distance. He learnt to connect my appearance with that of his food. I began to talk to him, calling him the first thing that came into my head: Black Boy.

One day as Black Boy approached I crouched down. I stretched my length on the lawn, almost lying on it as I reached towards him, holding my arm out. For one magical second he sniffed the tip of my finger. I immediately began a slow motion withdrawal so as not to alarm him. Slight though it, was that first voluntary contact was so rewarding.

As Spring changed into Summer I encouraged him to feed on the patio, nearer to the house. Little by little he got to tolerate me closer and closer. Then I touched him while he was feeding and he did not seem to mind. Soon I was stroking him all the while he ate.

He enjoyed human contact. After all, not every pet cat appreciates being stroked during his meals! But for Black Boy this was fine. Soon I could stroke him any time we met. I put my hands underneath him several times. Then I lifted him gently off the ground, just a foot or so and down again. He always seemed to be ready to accept the increased contact. Then I could pick him up and he was quite happy about this. By now it was September.

He became a most affectionate pet cat. He loved to be made a fuss of: he liked to be on my lap. In fact that year, as we watched the Last Night of the Proms on TV, Black Boy sat curled up on my lap the whole time.

In fact I have voted him as My Most Devoted Feline Follower. The only snag was that, in his efforts to stay with me, he did not always follow me. No, he was closer than that. He perfected that peculiarly feline art of walking between my feet when I tried to go down the garden path! He even began to play. Twice his attempts at an abrupt halt when running on the lawn resulted in a total pussy somersault. Head over heels he went landing momentarily on his back.

I was not aware of any problems between Black Boy and Spud and Sparkle. After all, they had probably seen more of him than I had since we first arrived. Having been an entire male until his mature years, (we never quite knew how mature!) he did have strong feelings about territory and such things and expressed these by occasionally peeing or pooing in the house during the day time even when he had ample access to the outdoor world. The solution appeared to be to put a large sheet of thick polythene in the two vulnerable areas, so at least I could clean up quickly and thoroughly.

So at first Black Boy came for food and frequented the house as he wished by day, but spent his nights wherever he had always spent them outside. Then a kind neighbour made a little hutch which we stood in what we call, rather too grandly, the courtyard. (No, it is not named after Hereford's theatre!) But the neighbour's fence, our fence including the gate to the carport, the kitchen wall and the greenhouse wall form a little quadrangle where we keep the dustbin and there was space enough there for Black Boy's hutch, where he could sleep when he chose. There was just room between the greenhouse and the neighbour's fence for me to squeeze through from the courtyard to the back garden, so there was ample access for a cat. I put suitable bedding in this hutch and Black Boy certainly did use it quite often.

But there was still the snag that if I heard a cat fight in the night, I would quickly put on my dressing gown and suitable footwear and go into the garden to call him and hopefully break up the fight. Black Boy was usually involved in these nocturnal battles, though there were a few occasions when both participants were other local cats. We had at least another couple of visits to the vet with an abcessed Black Boy! Prancing round the garden in the middle of the night, looking for a black cat in the dark is not my favourite occupation. Eventually I felt the time had come to keep him in at night along with Spud and Sparkle.

When we went away for a few days, we had a reliable friend to look after the cats. On our arriving home, Black Boy would be just inside the front door to greet us.

"I knew you were back home," the elderly lady next door said to us on one such occasion. "Black Boy was asleep in my garden. Suddenly he lifted up his head and listened and then made off to the fence at a gallop, or the best he could do for a gallop, as if to say, 'My folk are home and I must be there to greet them'". He made it in time.

So the cat whom we had first known as a frightened stray out in the garden spent the last three years or so of his life as a well loved pet.

Twinle, Queen of all she surveys

Chapter 7: Sharp Claws and a Piercing Squeak!

So we had Spud, Sparkle and Black Boy. Peter had been a bit reluctant about Black Boy's inclusion in our squad and three cats was felt to be pushing our limits somewhat, so we had no thoughts of getting any more. I was actively involved in the Cats' Protection shop at that time. When the main Cats' Protection fosterer had an Open Day it was interesting to go along and see the rescued cats who were awaiting re-homing.

The place was bulging with felines needing a home. I had a good look round though I do not have a clear memory of any of those in the outdoor pens. I had seen everything, or so I thought, when Peter made his big mistake.

"Come and look at these beautiful kittens", he said. I had not realised that there were a couple more cages in the garage. In the event I never did look in the second one of those.

The cage to which Peter had drawn my attention had on it a large notice, 'Kittens Booked'. Peter thought he was safe enough! What he had not realised was that the cage contained not three kittens, but two beautiful grey tabbies of eight weeks old and their diminutive grey kitten mother, no larger than they were. I put in my hand to touch one of the kittens and she promptly swiped me one with her paw for daring to approach her baby. (Perhaps she did not make full contact that time as there was no blood and in twelve years I have never known her swipe with claws retracted.)

Apparently a council worker had noticed the little grey cat on a farm in Ewyas Harold where she was struggling to look after her kittens in a hole somewhere. He had reported her plight to the Cats' Protection and so the little family had been brought into care. Their cage may have been small: all that was available at the time, but at least food was plentiful.

It was love at first sight. This tiny grey mother cat was so appealing. Her front legs were crooked as a result of early malnutrition. Her kittens were now being well fed and so was she, probably for the first time in her life She was not clearly marked tabby like her offspring, but a much more uniform grey with tabby markings on her face and tail and faintly on her legs. I cooed and drooled over her. I did not ask for her, as we had already exceeded the limit with three cats.

Then Peter said something I simply was not expecting, even from my ever-generous husband.

"Haven't you noticed that I didn't say, 'No'"? He had to say it twice for me to take it in!

We were due to go away on holiday in just over a couple of weeks' time so there was no immediate opportunity to settle in another cat. Eventually we agreed on something we both felt to be right. We would say nothing about having the grey puss. If she was still there in a month's time, we would ask for her and take it that it was right for us to have her. I must say that during that month I did pray that she would still be there for us.

I phoned as soon as we were back from holiday. Hurrah! She was still there. There had been enquiries after her, but they had not been followed up. Her kittens had gone to their home and she had been spayed. Life in that rather small cage was not ideal and we were glad to be able to go and collect her. We would have isolated her for a short while from the other cats while we got to know her a bit, but this became even more important as she had ear mites. Yes, she had some ointment for this, which I was to apply regularly.

I wanted to name her Minipuss, as she was quite the smallest cat I had seen. Peter objected to this. Giving way over a name was a small price to pay. After all, that gorgeous little grey cat, claws and all, was now mine, and that was what mattered. So we settled on Twinkle and as we got to know her, that name really suited her.

So Twinkle started off in my study, which would otherwise have been the third bedroom in our house. All our rooms are a decent size and at least she had a great deal more space than in the small cage she had been in since she was rescued.

We spent as much time with her as we could. We drank our morning coffee up in my study. Twinkle wanted to play rather than be petted. After all she had a lost kittenhood to catch up on. With the frequent visits we paid her, she really got to know us. It did not immediately stop her swiping at our hands with her extended claws whenever we moved a hand away from her. Peter wisely realised that if, when her claws struck, he kept his hand still, he could extricate himself without getting scratched. Also this gradually taught Twinkle not to react in this way or at least not to do so every time we touched her. Twelve years on we cannot totally rely on her not to take a swipe at us, but now she does it only very occasionally!

I had faithfully applied to her ears the ointment supplied by a vet before she was passed on to me though I was surprised that results from this seemed so slow. Within a couple of weeks we took her to our vet for a check-up and vaccination. He was horrified at the state of her ear mite infestation and gave her an injection to deal with this. He gave us instructions to continue to isolate her from other cats. She had another check up a fortnight later and then a further two weeks in the quarantine of my study before she was deemed mite free and fit to mix in feline society.

So the great day came when Twinkle was to meet Spud, Sparkle and Black Boy. They were all much bigger than she was and I was a bit apprehensive. If I had known her better then I would not have been. Twinkle walked into the living room where the three other cats were. They showed interest in investigating this intruder. Then Twinkle played her trump card. She rolled on her back, exposing her tummy, in a gesture of feline submission. The three other cats were taken in by this. Later on they would learn that she was anything but submissive, but for the moment this ploy had served her well.

In fact Twinkle does not make feline enemies. She accepts other cats and has her own ways of managing them to her advantage. But she never falls out with them or gets into a fight. If she wants a lap already occupied by a much larger cat, a bite on the tail or back leg of the occupier usually secures the lap for her. Very often now she has only to appear for the lap to be vacated for her.

She has a piercing squeak of a miaow. The other piercing aspects of Twinkle are, of course, her front claws. These are always needle sharp. She scratches posts and mats and all sorts, but never seems to shed outer sheaths off them as most cats do. In fact I generally have to clip the tips of her claws to prevent them just growing round into her pads. But this clipping never blunts them: nothing achieves that! Twelve years on they are still piercingly sharp and their owner is willing to use them on occasions! She often lies exposing her pretty soft tummy, but to touch it would risk getting one's hand shredded. When taking her annual blood test, the vet is always relieved if he has retained all his own blood! One lady vet, who was not at the practice for long, handled Twinkle somewhat carelessly and she was not so lucky!

But Twinkle is not vicious. She is a charming pet cat, loving attention and human company. She has a grunty little purr. She loves a lap, though she does then tend to dig her claws into one's knee. Eventually, after having little patterns of claw pricks on our knees repeatedly, we have got the idea of always putting enough padding of some sort between her and the knees!

She is a little beauty. She is short haired like all our cats. Her dense coat is very soft, almost like wool. Her underfur on her back and her tummy fur is either light grey, or beige or apricot, depending on the light. The tabby lines on her face give her all sorts of interesting expressions. Because of malnutrition in her youth, which I mentioned earlier, she had suffered from rickets. Thus she is bandy in front, the elbows of her front legs jutting out at an exaggerated angle. When she looks up and miaows she reminds one of a washerwoman with her arms akimbo! When she runs full speed the length of the lawn she looks like one of Thelwell's pony drawings! Yet her co-ordination is perfect: she never misses a jump onto furniture or even across the garden pond.

It was quite a time before I was happy to let her out in the garden and at first she had no idea about using the cat flap. She was so small. But I need not have worried. Anyway, her squeak could be heard most clearly, so there was no risk of her being left out when she really wanted to be in. After a while she did get the hang of the cat flap, which was quite an achievement as it was ideally placed for Sparkle, which meant it was head height for Twinkle. So much for those marvellous instructions on the box the cat flap was in when bought: measure your cat's clearance from the ground to find the right height for positioning the cat flap. What would you do if you had a Sparkle and a Twinkle, the long and the short in cat leg lengths? Even Spud could and did sometimes walk right under Sparkle, treating him as a kind of bridge.

Twinkle quite fancies herself as a hunter, though those short legs mean that when the intended prey is a bird, she has to take too many strides to have any hope of success. So the whole performance is good entertainment for her and any human audience, and good cat-avoidance practice for the bird, who is never endangered by these efforts.

On one occasion a female blackbird with newly fledged young took exception to Twinkle's presence in the garden. Twinkle, having dug her hole in my rock garden, was very properly relieving herself therein. Mrs. Blackbird flew up to her making the noises that offended blackbirds make, and she came low and struck Twinkle with her legs as she flew over. Twinkle fled. Victory to a very brave blackbird!

Twinkle has caught two mice in her twelve years with us. One, caught on Christmas Day, I managed to release unharmed. The other was less fortunate. But then there was also Mouse Number Three. I somehow suspected that there was a mouse under our freezer. Peter and I moved the freezer and the mouse ran out into the kitchen. We had both Twinkle and Lulu, the tortie you will read about later on, there with us. Between us we pursued a very evasive mouse. Then the mouse did a lap round the kitchen with Twinkle running beside it. She made no attempt to actually catch it. Eventually mouse disappeared through a small gap in the boarding by the side of the cooker. So, in the contest between two humans and two cats on one side and one mouse on the other, the mouse won!

In fact we had several mice in our understairs cupboard around this time. To add insult to injury they were eating the dry cat food stored there! I caught three or four and relocated them and Peter spent an uncomfortable couple of hours almost doubled up in the cupboard mouse-proofing it with fine wire mesh. To be fair to the cats they did not have access to that cupboard!

As far as I know Twinkle has only suffered one mishap in the garden, or should I say, the same mishap twice? I grew a most beautiful grass-like plant, Uncinia Rubra. Its leaves were a glowing bronzy red. But they were barbed. Twinkle began sneezing on and off, not enough to rush her to the vet, but after watching her for some days, we journeyed thither with her. Diagnosis was difficult at first. Then, when the vet had almost settled on some other cause of the problem, he noticed a tiny grass like protrusion from her nose. So it was an anaesthetic and the problem solved. Uncinia Rubra was the culprit. Twinkle had eaten it and it had got stuck in her throat and nose.

But it happened again. This time about two to three inches of Uncinia Rubra had got lodged in her throat and nose. The vet's surgery was not busy at just that time so it was dealt with there and then towards the end of the afternoon and I was presented with the offending item! I got home with a slightly dopey Twinkle.

As it was late in the year it was already dark. I took a torch so I could see what I was doing out in the garden and dug up all the plants of Uncinia Rubra I could find and consigned them to the compost heap. That was followed up by a ruthless policy with its many seedlings. So that was the second plant variety to be expelled from my garden for feline safety considerations.

Usually when we arrive home from any outing, we see all the cats within a few minutes of being back. One Sunday lunch time I could not find Twinkle. I called and called and was answered by that distinctive piercing squeaky miaow. But where was it coming from? Eventually I spotted her more than half way up one of the very tall conifers which still grew on the far side of the neighbour's garden. I had never known Twinkle climb a tree before, but with the motivation of a big black dog behind her, (it was with its owner who was on a visit next door) it was amazing what she could do! I was concerned that having got up, she would have difficulty getting down. Just as I had got the long step ladder out of the shed where we kept it, Twinkle arrived back in our garden none the worse for her adventure.

Twinkle spends a lot of her time out in the garden, but at least she does not wander far. Those short front legs mean that a garden fence is an insuperable barrier for her so she does not know there is a front garden and a road. She did sometimes go through the wire mesh fence down in the kitchen garden area and arrive in our neighbour's patch, though the presence of the resident dog was a discouragement to this. Our new fence has stopped that altogether. So it is generally easy to know where Twinkle is to be found. However, on a bright summer's evening when I call her to get her indoors, she has been known to head off into the border amongst the hostas and disappear from sight. Give her half an hour and then try again later! In the winter her outings are very brief.

Thatch in the kitchen

Chapter 8: A Prisoner Released

After Black Boy we were now reduced again to three cats. All three, Spud, Sparkle and Twinkle were affectionate pets and great characters. So we felt that this time we would be happy to take on a cat who simply needed a home, even if it turned out to be something of a passenger.

With this idea we set off to one of the Cats' Protection foster homes. Here a few cats were being cared for while it was hoped that homes for them would be forthcoming. One of them was a fifteen and a half year old white and tabby cat. His name was Thatch. For fifteen years he had been the Gloucester Prison Cat. He had come into Cats' Protection care as building operations at the prison had endangered his life and someone cared enough about him to pass him on to a safe place. I was told that the local media had taken an interest in his hand-over from the prison to the charity, but this had not generated interest

in re-homing him. He had already been with Cats' Protection for six months.

With the criteria we had worked out for selecting a cat, Thatch seemed to be a fairly obvious choice. Quite clearly he was not the kind of cat who would be quickly snapped up. So we decided that he was the cat for us.

We brought Thatch home and settled him into my study, the part of the house which was which was most suitable for settling in a new cat. Little by little we got to know him. He would tolerate being petted, though at first we never quite knew whether he liked it. Later on he seemed to enjoy it. He did not resist being handled, but tended to stiffen up. It was rather like picking up a fur covered wooden board! He was distinctly wary of feet, but considering his former home, it was not too difficult to guess why this could be.

When we let him wander around the house, we noticed that he did not seem to be using his toilet tray nearly as much as I would have anticipated. Small wonder then that soon after becoming aware of this, I realised that his preferred toilet was the carpet underneath Peter's computer table! (The vet's only comment on this was, "Be thankful that it was *under* the computer!") In fact it was to take much vigilance to compensate for Thatch's unwillingness to use the toilet trays.

When they met Thatch the other three cats did not appear bothered by his appearance on the scene and he showed no interest in them.

Once allowed out of doors Thatch would pace to and fro across the patio, to and fro and then up and down the garden path, like a prisoner on exercise. It must take some time to get used to freedom after fifteen years inside! Now that he had the run of the garden he developed the habit of using the middle of my plants, even some well established small shrubs, either as cat loos or as a beds for himself. Daphne Retusa, a very attractive little evergreen shrub with gorgeous pink flowers, was not improved by this treatment!

Peter and I discussed what to do about Thatch. Taking him back to Cats' Protection was not really an option. We did not want him to spend the rest of his life in a cage and who would want a fifteen and a half year old cat who appeared to be more or less indifferent to humans and sometimes behaved as if he was not house trained? So we decided we would persevere with him.

But as time went on he relaxed a bit. He gave up the pacing to and fro and took to wandering round our garden and next door's one too. He seemed less tense about being handled. Our vigilance compensated for his other failings aforementioned!

One September we were due to go on holiday and this was about the only time when we did not have anyone whom we could really ask to care for the cats, so we arranged for all of them to go to an excellent cattery. Two days before we were due to go, Thatch disappeared. I called and, though by this time he usually came to my call, there was absolutely no sign of Thatch. I enquired of neighbours and asked them to look in sheds and garages. I rang local vets' surgeries and the local RSPCA and Cats' Protection, but there was no news of Thatch whatever.

Peter could really do with the break so I decided the best way forward was to go on holiday as planned, leave the cat flap open, and ask the person who was going to keep an eye on the house to put fresh cat food down in the kitchen each day if there was any sign that it was being eaten.

I prayed a lot about Thatch during that holiday. On our way home we collected the other cats from the cattery and I got indoors and went straight to the kitchen. Cat food had been eaten from the dish I had left there. Yes, Thatch was back! In fact, when I checked with the lady who had come into the house each day, he had come back the first day of our holiday! Thank you, Lord!

We got fond of Thatch during the four years he was with us. I think he got vaguely affectionate! During a check up at the vets he was found to have thyroid problems, but since no little tumour was showing itself, this was to be corrected by tablets rather than surgery. So Thatch was to be given a pill each day, and he accepted this with little resistance.

Some time later on, I noticed that the pupils of his eyes were constantly dilated and my own checks on him led me to suppose he had become blind. So we had another visit to the vet which confirmed my suspicions. But in an environment which he already knew, this was not a problem for Thatch. It was more of a problem for us, as we wanted to know that he could always find a litter tray, or the outside world, when he needed this.

I put up a cardboard barrier to prevent him from penetrating into the house further than the kitchen, where he had a bed by the radiator. The trouble was that we had to step over this barrier every time we went in or out of the kitchen! Thatch still had access to the back garden and this was quite safe for him with no chance of him finding his way to the road. He seemed content enough.

When we had a few days' break, Thatch lodged at the vets where he was well known and would have excellent care. However, the change of routine and surroundings left him so disorientated for a while afterwards that I decided this must not be repeated. So next time we left him at home with the others and our good friend, who now cared for the cats in our absence, looked after him too.

He did sometimes manage to get further into the house than the kitchen and a favourite place was in the bathroom under the radiator. On returning from holiday we found Thatch in the kitchen and a ceramic Thatch in his choice place in the bathroom. That sort of thing can happen when you have artistic friends!

Lulu in a box in the greenhouse

Chapter 9: A Hedgehog's Legacy

Most summers we have a hedgehog of two in the garden. One summer evening I went down the garden at dusk wearing open sandals and a young hedgehog came up to me as I stood still. To my amusement he checked with his teeth as to whether my big toe was edible. I did not leave it in range for further investigation, just in case the verdict was positive. I often put cat food out at night when I knew there were hedgehogs around.

I was concerned when I found a small hedgehog one autumn. He looked to be too small to hibernate safely. I fed him regularly. In the tiny quadrangle between the two fences, the greenhouse and our house there was still the little hutch which the kind neighbour had given us as a shelter for Black Boy before he settled in the house. The prickly little fellow soon discovered the access to this from the garden by going between the fence and the greenhouse. When I filled this hutch with

straw the hedgehog moved in. So it was easy to put food within a couple of feet of his chosen bed.

Throughout the winter I kept a saucer with cat food on it near the hutch. Hogpig would snooze for a few days and then emerge to feed. He did have one longer sleep of about three weeks. One night we had a sprinkling of snow and there were his tiny footmarks imprinted in it, leading from his front door to the saucer of food and back to the hutch!

Hogpig got through the winter safely. Up until the end of March or early April I saw him from time to time and was still feeding him. Then one day when I looked out into the tiny courtyard, there was a tortoiseshell and white cat eating the food.

"If it's someone's pet having a snack, she will soon move on", I thought.

So I put out more food. She ate that too. She had had enough to satisfy any normal cat, so I thought that she must have gone and put out yet more food. She ate that as well.

Light began to dawn. "That cat has eaten eight ounces of food straight off! She isn't someone's pet. She must be starving."

If a hungry cat had at last found food, I did not feel like cutting off the supply. So I began putting food out for this tatty tortoiseshell cat. She hung around the place. I placed an old dustbin on its side in the

little courtyard and put some rags in it as bedding and she immediately moved in as if to say, "At last I've got somewhere to call my own!"

She has white paws, chest and tummy. On the rest of her coat the ginger and black are not symmetrical and at times they merge together. Her tail is small and short. A bigger, longer one would suit her better. But the one she has got has a white mark one side towards the tip, which makes it look as though she had encountered a loaded paint brush. When we first saw her, her coat was in very poor condition, patchy and largely missing on her back towards her tail.

She was a little nervous, but on my first attempt to stroke her, she allowed this. She was certainly regular in attendance for meals. In fact she was usually in her dustbin! A small advertisement in the local shop produced no reply from her former owners. She looked as though they had lost all interest in her some good while back!

I wanted to call her Pusscat. Peter suggested Lulu, after the disreputable heroine in Alban Berg's unfinished opera of that name. She certainly looked the part! By the time I took her to the vet for a check-up and vaccination, we had not yet resolved the name so she was at first registered as LP. However, she was soon known as Lulu.

Lulu was both friendly and nervous at the same time. She was not helped by Sparkle's determination to see her off the premises! With regular feeding her coat improved, until she looked quite respectable. However, for a few years after this, she would fur chew from time to time, generally spoiling her slightly fluffy trousers. On the whole her coat felt coarser than that of our other cats, and it tended to stand up slightly more than theirs.

So Lulu joined our feline squad. As with Black Boy, a few months passed before I got her in at nights, but once I had done so, she settled to this new routine. It was quite clear that Lulu was a young cat, maybe about two years old. She was tremendously agile and would spend ages chasing leaves on the lawn. She could leap up six feet onto the fences with the greatest of ease.

Later on one frosty morning Lulu amused herself on the ice of the garden pond, dancing around and patting at the goldfish who were moving about under the ice. Her paws kept skidding in all directions.

On another occasion the ice was somewhat thinner. I did not actually see what happened. What I did see was a hole in the ice in the middle of the pond. On the frosty lawn there were a couple of wet patches, about the distance apart that a startled cat could leap. Of Lulu, who was normally around at that time, there was no sign. My guess is that she was licking herself dry somewhere under the shrubs.

Lulu is a scatty cat. She really would not rank very high in a feline IQ test! If there was trouble in the form of Sparkle, she had a knack of walking into it. If I was around she would look up to me to be rescued:

that is, lifted up out of it. This is even more so now that we have taken on Tigger and Teazle, two tabbies who also disliked her on sight.

She was easy enough to handle once she had come into the house, but unlike all our other cats, quite difficult to catch if she was in the garden. It was often a case of luring her through the door and then shutting it behind her. Fine when I managed it, but often she would get spooked just as she was about to come in and off she would dash. Then I need to leave it around half an hour before trying again. In spite of that she has not had a night out since she became a full furry member of the household. Nowadays she is usually already in the house by the time I want to shut the cats indoors. Otherwise she is less reluctant to be caught now if she happens to be out in the garden.

Most cats who come onto one's lap, curl up, or stretch out in a position comfortable for both parties. Not Lulu, or at least not often! Sometimes she will come and stand on my lap, resisting all efforts to encourage her to fold her legs up. More often she will stand half on me and half on the arm of the chair or settee. Whatever I am doing, knitting, crocheting or reading, Lulu arrives as the perfect sabotage pack!. Perhaps she will only stay for two or three minutes, but then she will repeat the performance half a dozen times in the evening, unless my lap is already occupied and that deters her.

Sometimes in her chosen place around the house Lulu curls up in a ball and sometimes she sits up tidily with her feet in a row, but when she lies down her position is often unusual for a cat. Instead of tucking all four paws neatly underneath and ending up in a sort of rectangle as most cats do, Lulu will stretch her two front legs right out and cross one over the other.

For the first few years with us, Lulu remained rather shy of anyone but myself. Then we had a young friend, Sue, staying with us for three months. Her back was injured and while with us she could rest a lot and be in company. Sue and Lulu spent hours together and both benefited from this. Sue, who had been allergic to cats, got over this to a large extent. Lulu was probably the first cat she had really got to know well. She later adopted several rescued cats and put the 'blame' for this on Lulu. Lulu was helped by the hours of human company and attention and became much more confident with people. After that three month period Sue was often with us from time to time and Lulu always remembered her. She still does.

One day Sue came in from the garden to tell me that Lulu was playing with something under the kitchen window. I went out to have a look, saw a thick rodent tail disappearing amongst the plants, so I removed Lulu and got a pair of gloves. Parting the vegetation I picked up a silver grey gerbil! It was completely unharmed: perhaps Lulu had never even caught it. Anyway, if she had not done so, I had and now there was the question of what to do with it.

We were lent a small cage which tided us over till I could buy it a larger one. We tried in vain to find its owner, but when we discovered how it could bite, we began to think that its wanderings may not have been the result of an escape on its part. Sue took it home with her, named it Squirrel, and it lived out a fairly normal gerbil lifespan. It was often reasonable to handle, but one never quite knew when one would feel those rodent teeth.

Eventually after having had five cats, we were reduced to two again. Spud and Thatch had both made it into their twentieth year. Then we were left with just Twinkle and Lulu. I think Lulu regarded this as the golden age of her time with us. She could cope with Twinkle more or less. But the golden age did not last long: we took on two more tabbies.

On one occasion during this golden age Sue was standing out in the garden and she saw Lulu and Twinkle by the pond. In fact, Twinkle was drinking from the pond, and that meant leaning into it a long way for her because of those short front legs. Lulu bounced up to Twinkle and gave her a wallop on her behind and sent her flying into the middle of the shallow end of the pond. Twinkle stood there for a moment in sheer astonishment. "How did I get here?" she seemed to be wondering. Then she shot out of the pond and disappeared in the border.

A few years on, Lulu lost condition somewhat in the summer and began to look like an old cat. Of course, our idea of her age was only a guess from the energy she displayed when we first took her on. Come the winter and she had picked up again and I forgot about her summer low until the following year when it was all considerably more pronounced. Lulu was now not eating at all well and she was losing weight fast. Our usual vet, who knew her, was on holiday and the one who saw her twice did not pick up that anything was wrong.

At the very first opportunity I took her to the vet who knew her. He gave her a thorough once over and discovered a tell-tale nodule on the front of her neck, almost certainly an indicator of thyroid problems. He took a blood test to check this and sent it off. Next day he rang with the results: Lulu's thyroxin levels were as high as he had ever seen and so he would operate on her the next day.

It took Lulu two of three days to recover from the operation and begin to get her appetite back again. But that treatment turned her round completely. Her condition picked up rapidly and she no longer looked old, in fact she became quite a stocky, plump pussy, but not over-fat. She is certainly no longer as quick and fast as when we first knew her, but that is good news for the birds.

Though she does not look old, she must be at least thirteen by now. She no longer wears her claws down and she does not like my having a look at them. In fact she will give me a gentle warning bite if I do. I need to do more than look at them: I need to clip them or they will curl round into her pads. Fortunately I have an old Elizabethan collar, that thing like a clear plastic flower pot with no bottom, which another cat wore after his first operation. When I put that on Lulu, she stands and purrs helplessly and I can clip all her claws without any real protest from her.

Lulu is sometimes to be found either behind the settee, under the spare bed, or on a cushion on the kitchen table. (I once made the mistake of briefly placing this old cushion on the kitchen table and it had become a favoured cat bed before I decided where else to put it.) For Lulu the vital thing is to be out of range of the tabby cats, who are liable to attack her. Often I carry her downstairs after she has been imprisoned upstairs for hours by a tabby guard on the landing.

Her language fending off these enemies is very expressive and maybe excessive as well. It is a bit like having one's own private domestic thunderstorm. She flattens her ears till you would hardly know she has any. In vain I tell her that she was the one who chose to join a multi-cat household. But for all her problems with tabbies, she sticks to the house like a limpet, rarely going more than half way down the garden. After all, there is food and warmth, shelter and affection to be found here.

Teazle relaxes on the carpet

Chapter 10: Two Tabby Friends

So there was a brief period one autumn when we had only two cats, Lulu and Twinkle. Five had certainly been rather many for us, but with only two, I was now wanting another cat. After all, three would be fine!

A friend rang to ask if I had any suggestions as to how she could re-home her two cats as, much as she loved them, she could no longer keep them since she had developed an allergic reaction to them. I offered what ideas I could, though in the event none of them produced anything. We only wanted one cat and my friend was clear that these two were friends and must be homed together.

But we were not finding our new cat and my friend was not finding a home for her two tabbies, Tommy and Timmy. We agreed to go and see them. I have never conducted a feline interview before and judging from results I was not much good at it! We had a pleasant evening,

but for some reason Peter and I were totally unimpressed with the two cats. There was nothing to put us off them. They were obviously in fine condition, used to being pets, but we simply had not been attracted to them.

We talked it over on the phone with our friends. We agreed that over the next six weeks we would all pray for a good home for the two tabbies. If that had not been found elsewhere by the end of November, then we would conclude that it was to be with us.

No, by the end of November, Tommy and Timmy had no new home. So it was time for action. As one of the cats was on some medication at that time, our friends kept them for a further week, until the condition was cleared. up. Then they would come to us. So I got my study ready to receive two rather large cats.

Our friends brought the two tabbies to us in the morning of the first Saturday in December. The cats could not quite make out what was happening and why they had been moved into a smallish room, but they were so very friendly and placid about it all. Why had not I taken to these two cats when I first saw them? I cannot answer that one, but I certainly took to them in a big way now that they were mine. They are an adorable pair.

On the whole I prefer not to use human names for my animals. So Tommy was renamed Tigger. He is a tall, long-legged, long tailed, tabby and white cat, with clear markings. When he curls himself up, he usually has an untidy heap of paws left over! Theoretically they are white paws with black pads, but washing them has never been his strong point and so those big paws are usually various shades of distinctly off-white. Tigger has some white on his tummy and some gingery fur there too as well as tabby. He also has a white chest. But it is his half white nose which gives him a somewhat quizzical look and that suits his character so well. He had had a road accident when he was quite young and still has a pin in one back leg, but this causes him no trouble.

Those paws of his might be grubby, but they are handy! If his friend was eating something Tigger fancied, Tigger could not get his face in the dish, but he could hook something out on his paw and do quite well that way. He has developed a habit of sloshing his drinking water all over the kitchen floor with one of those big paws. He often likes to have a paw in the water while he drinks. Well, there can be no accounting for tastes. When he drinks from the garden pond, then there is some point in his paddling the duck weed away before he actually drinks, though he tends to paddle the water whether there is any weed there or not.

On one occasion when Tigger was on my lap while Peter and I sat on the settee watching snooker on BBC 2, suddenly the channel was changed. Neither of us had moved. We looked at one another. Then we realised that it was Tigger who had his paw on the remote control!

Tigger loves attention and particularly has developed the habit of joining us at mid-morning for his coffee cuddle as we call it. When he is in really purry mood, the more he is cuddled the better he likes it. But he does have an over-active ending: he can be purring happily on my lap on our settee and slapping Peter with his tail at the same time. If his tail is still that is often a sign that he is asleep!

Teazle was the name I chose for Timmy. Apart from under his chin, where he does have some white normally hidden from view, he is tabby all over. This is much less clearly marked than Tigger's coat and in fact a different colour. It is a bit more sandy than the colour of a wild rabbit, in fact his tummy is almost light ginger. He has faint black stripes, so he is a sort of mackerel tabby. These stripes do become more pronounced on his chest, his legs, down his back and especially on his tail. If its length were doubled, that tail would do well for a lemur. The fur under his paws is black and this black finish really looks good when one has the chance to see it. He is a shorter, stockier cat than Tigger, though he tends to be the heavier of the two. Currently he weighs seven kilos. I am sure he felt relieved when the vet said that though he is overweight, he is not dangerously so.

When Twinkle and Lulu were out, I let Tigger and Teazle explore the house. That way the cats would get each others' scent before they actually met. The first time I did this Teazle discovered a ten kilo bag of Feline Maintenance at the bottom of the stairs and he wasted no time in chewing through both layers of the bag and helping himself. Although they had been used to tinned food, these new boys soon put themselves onto Feline Maintenance as at least half their diet!

In the early days Teazle would jump on to the work top in the kitchen if he suspected that I had left anything edible there. I always say the pussy prayer is "Lead us not into temptation!", so it was up to me to see that nothing enticing to Teazle was left where it could be reached.

During these early explorations of the house, Teazle discovered what was clearly a dangerous beastie, which must be approached with the greatest care. In fact it was the coiled lead to the telephone. Teazle's fur bristled and he stalked it with the utmost caution, ready to flee if it sprang at him. Eventually after about ten minutes he was near enough to give it a pre-emptive dab with his paw. It did not retaliate! So he gave it another whack. That convinced him he had eliminated the danger.

After a little while, the four cats met each other in the house, without incident and at least got used to the idea that all four belonged here. It was not till a bit later that both new tabbies made it quite clear that they objected to Lulu. Poor Lulu, I do not think tabby is her favourite colour.

Tigger is a very vocal cat. He starts chirruping before he ever arrives at the cat flap. Many of his movements in the house are announced with a chirrup. On the other hand, when we remove him from a chair, or pick him up, he frequently grizzles! I love that little grizzle and quite miss it when he omits it. Not that Tigger would dream of expressing his objection more strongly: he appears to have a firm conviction that claws were not made to be used on humans. But at times he is not even quiet when asleep!

He is also a lively cat, living with enthusiasm. This reminds me of A.A. Milne's rhyme about Tigger seeming bigger because of his bounces.

Early on in their time with us there came a day when half way through the morning I thought to myself, 'Where is Tigger?' I had not seen him for three hours. Maybe that is not long, but already the two tabbies, like our other cats, were rarely away for more than an hour or so at a time. I called, but no Tigger came. Then I searched the house. Behind a chair in the spare bedroom, there was a very sorry Tigger. He cried if I touched him: clearly he was in pain. I rang the vet and was told Tigger would be seen immediately I brought him down.

A complete examination would have been too painful, so Tigger was given anti-inflammatory and anti-biotic injections and I was to phone in on his progress at twelve hourly intervals over the Bank Holiday. He began to recover almost immediately. When I took him for a check-up a close examination showed puncture wounds all over his chest. Clearly he had been in a fight and come off rather badly and had developed an infection as a result of the bites he had received.

Teazle is the champion purrer. To purr is his solution to many situations. And what a purr that is, quite the loudest I have heard. He often starts up if I so much as speak to him and he can keep it up for ages, a lovely comfortable sound. Apart from that, he was a silent cat for his first year with us, at least so long as he did not meet the opposition.

Teazle took upon himself the defence of territory. This led to constant duels with a big black and white cat. It also led to frequent visits to the vet so all the staff at the surgery knew Teazle and knew why he has had to come in to them so frequently. One vet advised him to hang up his boxing gloves or learn to do it better. Another after treating him, had a sympathetic conversation with him about territory and boundaries and the responsibility of being the only one who cared about such things.

On one occasion I saw and heard both Teazle and the Enemy on top of next door's garden shed. They were out of range of any jet of water I could aim, so there was nothing I could do except watch and listen. There was Teazle on the ridge of the shed, with his mouth open, hurling feline abuse at the black and white puss, who was doing a slow motion backwards retreat away from him. Their meeting on this occasion did not come to blows. Teazle sang, or rather caterwauled his enemy off the shed roof. On a much later occasion they met in the neighbour's conifer which overhangs our fence and I managed to lean over and extract Teazle. No, I did not get scratched. Teazle, like his friend Tigger, is also a sweet tempered cat.

About a year after he came to us, Teazle developed a lump on his tummy and this had to be removed. For a few days he wore an Elizabethan collar, (the one I now find handy for Lulu) and was confined to the spare bedroom. He simply took to one of the beds and enjoyed his convalescence.

One day, after Tigger and Teazle had been with me for about a year, Teazle miaowed to me for the first time. It was not the kind of miaow one expected from a cat of his size. After that he would use his miaow on rare occasions and gradually these have got more frequent. He will call to me if he was responding to my call. He has even got quite chatty. Then I accidentally shut him in the garden shed and he was there for about five hours. When I could not find him and called him, his reply did let me know exactly what he thought of this accidental incarceration! He was so pleased to be let out, he purred and purred and purred.

Tigger and Teazle remain good friends. Theirs is the only example of a feline friendship amongst my cats so far. While they do not curl up together in one furry heap, they certainly like being near each other. They are very frequently in the same room or the same part of the garden, or both snoozing on the old carpet which is on top of the compost heap. Whenever they meet they usually greet each other with a gentle head butt. This is often followed by one licking the other's head. They have mock battles, usually initiated by Tigger. Sometimes Teazle looks a bit bored with these, or wants to opt out sooner than Tigger does.

One day Tigger and Teazle attacked Lulu in next door's garden, just by the neighbour's open kitchen door. George, the neighbour's big, bouncy, black Labrador rushed outside with many woofs to see what was happening on his patch and the cats scattered and then the three of them all arrived indoors. Lulu, the victim, seemed the least perturbed and sat on the kitchen table licking herself. She had come to no harm. The two tabbies seemed a bit shaken by the whole experience.

It was some hours later that we realised we had not seen Tigger again since he came in the house. I called, but no Tigger. I searched the house, under the spare bed, in the wardrobe, behind the chairs, but still no Tigger. No Tigger outside either. Periodically I called and searched, but when night came there was no sign of him indoors or out.

I wanted to leave the cat flap open so Tigger could get into the kitchen during the night. So I put Teazle and Twinkle, who usually share the kitchen and the adjacent greenhouse with him at night, into the spare bedroom. So they had their food, water and cat loos up there for the night.

Needless to say I was up earlier than usual next morning. First I checked the kitchen. No sign of Tigger and no evidence that he had been in: the food was untouched. Better let the other cats out and then print out a notice asking neighbours to look in sheds, garages, etc. So I opened the spare bedroom door and out walked Twinkle and Teazle .... and Tigger! When I had searched for him, I had not looked under the chest of drawers in the spare bedroom as it had not dawned on me that such a long-legged cat could fold himself up under that and stay there for at least ten hours! But Tigger could and here he was, safe and sound, and he had had all facilities and his friends with him overnight!

That day Tigger certainly put his tail between his legs when he next heard George bark, but he calmed down as the day progressed and was none the worse for his adventure. Unfortunately it did nothing to improve his attitude to Lulu. What Tigger did not realise is that George would never hurt a cat anyway.

A favourite summer pastime for all the cats is frogging. This means locating any innocent frog who was hoping for a quiet day under a shady plant. It is then sniffed or patted into action. As the frog hops, the cat follows, but never too close as that unpredictable hop clearly adds an element of risk to the game from the pussy point of view. After a bit the frogs mainly deal with the situation in one of two different ways. One is to make for one of the two ponds as fast as hops will take them. The other is to freeze completely still until the cat loses interest. I do not know of a frog who has been hurt by the cats' frogging as they do not use their claws at all for this. A few unfortunates have been brought indoors by Tigger, but I have been able to release them quickly. Fortunately I like frogs and am quite happy handling them. This is true of most of the beasties I might meet in the garden.

One damp summer's day, when the patio door into the living room was wide open, the cats' body language said, "There is a frog under the settee". I moved the settee and there was the frog. It had been a tadpole a very short time ago. It could have sat on my thumb nail with room to spare, but it had suffered no harm from its adventure.

After Tigger had been with me a good seven years, he was diagnosed with thyroid problems, as Lulu had been. This had affected his heart and he was tending to flop down anywhere, presumably when he ran out of steam. Fortunately he was a case where the thyroid problem was dealt with by an operation.

A little while after this he had his blood pressure checked. He heart was doing better, but his blood pressure was too high. So Tigger is now on daily medication for high blood pressure. One pill which he has is palatable anyway. He also has one eighth part of another pill and this I conceal in a minute amount of cheese. So he regards his daily dose as a little evening treat. I take care that the cheese he has is only around the size of a small pea, just in case there might be digestive problems if it were larger. This regime keeps our Tigger fit and healthy.

Tigger drinking with his right paw in the water

Tommy Primrose

Chapter 11: A Promise Redeemed

In our early days in Hereford there was a lady named Margaret Primrose amongst the folk in a house group bible study which I was leading . She told me that she was taking on a young cat. His owners, who were in the forces, had been posted to Cyprus, so their cat had to be re-homed. There was the complication that his face had been badly smashed in a recent road accident. The vet had done a good job. But the cat's right eye was so badly damaged the only way forward was to take it out. His jaw was wired up until a break there mended. The cat's name was Tommy.

I did not see Tommy until he was fully fit again. From time to time when I visited Margaret I ended up with the job of giving Tommy his flea treatment or his worm pill. When he was poorly in any way, it was often I who decided whether he needed a visit to the vet after Margaret

had a chat with me over the phone. Then Margaret would come round and borrow a cat basket in which to transport him.

One day Margaret expressed her concern to be sure there was someone to care for Tommy if she became unwell or had to go into a residential home. This did not appear to be imminent as she was in good health at that time, but she was about ten or twelve years older than ourselves. Peter and I discussed the matter and agreed to promise Margaret that if she had to part with Tommy we would do our best to settle him in with our squad.

When Tommy was eight years old Margaret's health went downhill to such an extent that she decided to sell her house and go into a residential home. So it was time for us to take on Tommy. We were just about to go on holiday, so a neighbour fed him for a couple of weeks. Then we went to collect him. He was not in Margaret's house or garden. But when I called, he replied vocally and trotted up to us, tail high. When I put him in the cat basket and into our car, he yowled and complained that he had been kidnapped!

He is quite a stocky cat, with shortish legs and a very broad chest. The way his tail can bend over his back reminds me of the handle of one of those milk jugs made in the shape of a cow; Tommy is the perfect model for the cat version. Is he tabby and white, or black and white with tabby edgings to the black? A lot of his fur is black all through, unlike a tabby's fur. The back of his head and the whole of his back are black; in some positions viewed from the back, he can look like a black cat. But the black is edged with tabby. He has quite a generous amount of white on his paws, his chest, tummy and nose, but right at the end of his nose he has a tabby patch. Looks a bit like a moustache In fact if Tommy Primrose had been human he definitely would have been a retired officer from the armed forces. His whole manner says that!

Tommy is always meticulous about cleanliness. If his paws have got clogged with mud while he is busy digging up my garden, he will sit in the living room and clean between his pink pads, dropping little dobs of mud on the carpet. His white parts are always well laundered, shining white. Perhaps he is an advert for a superior brand of cat lick!

I decided that his former surname suited him, so his full name remains Tommy Primrose.

He has a wide range of miaows. These range at one end from a commanding yowl, often addressed to recalcitrant humans and at the other a gorgeous gruff "Thank you" when he has been obliged. I soon realised that he was a bossy, bully cat and it would not do to give way to him. However, when he sees that he is not going to get his own way in any matter, he does usually submit graciously!

At first he had an unfortunate habit of attacking one's ankles, not often, but now and then. A combination of making loud disapproving noises and being watchful has got him out of that one, to my relief, as they were always my ankles which were attacked. Further beware of that tempting tummy, so often exposed as he likes to lie completely upside down, paws in the air and tail neatly curled between his back legs. At first when I wanted to pick him up the only safe thing to do was first to roll him over with my foot, ignore the protests and get him firmly on his paws before putting my hands to him. In those early days I reckoned he needed a 'Handle with care' notice attached to him. But he has mellowed with the passing of time and become thoroughly amenable to handling now and apparently enjoys it.

Soon after taking him on we were away again, so before he could be let out he had a few days confined to the spare bedroom where he was well looked after by the friend who cared for the cats in our absence. Since he had only moved about a mile, I was particularly keen to get him microchipped, in case there was a risk of his returning to old haunts, or worse still, getting lost on the way. Now as I write we have had Tommy over five years. Yes, he has been out of our back garden, but only as far as the next door back garden! Now we have a new fence he does not go out of our garden. He is the most stay at home tom cat we have ever had!

Altogether Tommy was with us a month before I let him out of doors. During that month I tried to supervise his meetings with our other cats. How does one know that introducing a heavyweight neutered tom to others of the same ilk will be all right? It was certainly the subject of much prayer. When he met Tigger and Teazle around the house, I would sit on the floor beside them. They certainly did not take to each other, but there were no untoward incidents. Nevertheless I was prepared to be watchful during that first outing and my attention was divided between the garden and the cats.

All went well at first and then Teazle went up to Tommy. My interpretation of the body language of the two cats was this.

Teazle, "Let's have it out now!"

Tommy, "Thank you, but I don't fight!"

Certainly Tommy's attitude saved the day. If the toms had started fighting then, there would have been no way that we could have kept Tommy Primrose.

A little later on that day Tommy dug his first hole in our garden. He is an expert digger. He must have friends in Australia, whom he is trying hard to contact. I want to say that a well-aimed pawful of earth went straight in Teazle's face! However, I think that is reading into the situation an intention which was not there. But it did look funny as a sequel to Teazle's challenge.

Teazle and Tommy have settled for making rude noises at each other when one wants to pass the other and taking an occasional swipe at each other when opportunity offers, but mercifully nothing worse than that. With Tigger, Tommy has the upper paw, and will chase him down the garden, but Tigger is built for speed in a way that Tommy never was.

Tommy Primrose is a cat with definite likes and dislikes. As far as food goes, he simply likes it, lots of it. Time and again we have threatened to rename him Tummy. The family in the house adjoining ours put out white bread for the birds. The birds then often drop bits of it on our lawn or garden and Tommy falls on this as if it were manna from heaven. Scraps of food that I put out for the birds on our lawn go down the same way. We have such hoards of tadpoles in the nearer of the two garden ponds that I often feed them on fish food or brown bread in May and June. Tommy spends ages leaning precariously over the edge of the pond, pawing the water as he tries to get a morsel of this to come his way.

Tommy Primrose eats more grass than any cat I have ever known, but almost always appears to digest it: certainly it is extremely rare for him to bring it up again. For Tommy a daily graze is a must.

The term 'bedding plant' clearly means one thing for a human and another for a cat. There are one or two of my perennials which Tommy finds particularly comfortable. One prostrate member of the broom family is growing on the rock garden and I would like to remove it and put something more interesting to me there, but no, it is one of Tommy's favourite sunshine resorts.

When we only had a wire mesh fence down the lower part of the garden, Tommy would occasionally go into the garden next door. On one occasion, George, the big Labrador bounced up to him, "Woof, woof, woof!" Tommy's whole attitude said, "So what?" and he sat tight where he was while George came to an embarrassed halt about three feet away.

I get the cats indoors before dark and there they stay, with all needed facilities, until the morning. There is only one exception to this, namely Tommy Primrose. I can let him out in the dark and usually rely on him to be back at the back door in ten minutes. (I set the oven timer so that I do not forget him!)

On the rare occasions when he is not already back, he comes to a call, trotting up the garden path. His speed depends on the weather: he can do quite a fast trot in sleet! But if there are a lot of frogs about he can get distracted, and then it is a question of just going out and picking him up. Once I wondered what had happened to his whiskers while he was out, as he returned with some additions to these. Yes, he had something else there besides his whiskers: the legs of a frog held gently in his mouth and deposited as soon as he got inside the greenhouse. I saw to it that it was outside again in minutes.

Are we the only household with a fridge lock on the shower door put there to prevent a cat from opening it and walking in with muddy paws? Tommy Primrose developed the habit of hooking the shower door open with one movement of his paw. (So much for the magnetic seal!) Then he would pad round the shower and lick its base. Peter had an interesting time in Mothercare explaining what kind of fridge lock we needed and why. No, it was not grandchildren, (of whom, of course, we have none) raiding the fridge, but a cat opening the shower door. The fridge lock has defeated him, but he has not given up trying in the two years it has been there.

After we had Tommy for just over three years, he began to lose weight rather too quickly and he was drinking a phenomenal amount of water. Whereas previously he had rarely if ever used an indoor toilet tray, he was now spending outsize pussy pennies in it twice a night. He had a visit to the vet for a diagnosis of his problem and we were told that he had become diabetic. I asked how this would affect his life expectancy and was told it would not make any difference. So Tommy started on one insulin injection a day.

That proved to be insufficient. He had two or three visits to the vet before he was finally stabilised on two injections a day. No cat could be easier to inject. I just push him into the best position to get a good handful of the scruff of his neck and he seems to understand what

I want. He is so incredibly obliging about all this. I must say I get more and more fond of him day by day as he accepts his injections so amiably. Very frequently he just purrs!

Tommy is not a cat who will jump up onto a lap, in fact he and Thatch are the only cats I have had not do so. But he does like a fuss and cuddle and will rub round my legs in the kitchen till I pick him up and have five minutes sitting with him and fussing him.

He has taken on the role of Feline Traffic Warden in our household, stationing himself at one doorway or another, so he can swear at the other cats as they pass by him. We do tend to get the cat flap picketed with one cat either side daring the other to attempt to use it. It is amazing how often Tommy Primrose is the picket.

Sooty

Chapter 12: The Little Black Cat.

Not many of the neighbouring cats parade our garden: Teazle, our territorial tabby, sees to that. With five resident moggies we did think that it was adequately populated. But in the summer of 2003 a little black cat began to show considerable interest in food put out for either birds or the hedgehog. She appeared nervous, ready to flee if she saw me and this was not helped by my own cats who half-heartedly chased her off, well for a few yards anyway.

I looked at her through binoculars and she did not appear to be in too bad condition. But she was hungry, so after a while I began to put out food for her. Where had she come from? Was she a feral cat, or an abandoned pet?

At the bottom of the garden a very tall conifer hedge screens us from the nearby council estate. Under this hedge is a junk area where anything from the garden which needs to go to the dump waits for our

rather infrequent trips in that direction. Whatever will compost goes on the compost heap, but even the most enthusiastically green person would not be able to compost a broken down metal wheel-barrow!

One day I decided to do some tidying up in that area and almost as soon as I began the little black cat leapt out of the junk with an expression which might have said, "But this is the only home I have now".

As she prepared to disappear over the fence I spoke to her and she paused and three times answered me with a scarcely voiced miaow. That conversation with her told me quite a bit. No, she was not feral. She was a little cat who, given the chance, would respond to humans. She had a home once. Needless to say the tidying up under the hedge stopped there.

Autumn replaced summer and I was concerned that little black cat should not have to face Guy Fawkes' bangs out of doors. She was now sleeping under the discarded wheel-barrow on a bed I had improvised for her. But the Cats' Protection shelter was full. She could go on the waiting list, but they could not help until some uncertain time in the future.

When I discussed this with a friend, she said, "But think of a black cat at the back of a cage!" No one chooses a black cat as people tend to go for the pretty ones. That remark did make me think.

One day towards the end of October, as I was taking out her food, I saw the little black cat walking up the garden path. That was awkward as she usually made off when she saw me. How could I get the food dish down for her without frightening her away? I walked towards the opposite side of the lawn, so both puss and I would be going diagonally across the lawn, heading for the same point, but not walking directly towards each other. All the time I continued speaking to her, naming her Sooty as the first thing that came into my head.

Did I say I walked? I crouched as low as I could so as not to scare her. No, I did not crawl: one does not do that in one's late sixties! (I guess I could have done, but remember, we do have neighbours!) To keep my balance I had to concentrate on where I was going and so took my eyes off the cat. I carefully placed the dish of food on the lawn and began to withdraw very, very slowly, so slowly that before I had done so, a little black head thrust itself into my hand. That was one of those unforgettable moments. She rubbed and wrapped herself round my legs and just could not get enough fuss and stroking. For once, food could wait!

From that moment we were firm friends. Sooty, as I had instantly called her, simply loved being petted and handled. She was not even bothered a few days later when I took her in the car to our vet's surgery to be checked for a microchip. The receptionist gave her a quick once over. No microchip.

"I'll just have a look at her teeth", she said. As she opened Sooty's mouth she gave a gasp, "No teeth!"

Some one had taken care of her when she had problems with her teeth or gums. But she was not on any of the four Lost and Found Registers I enquired about, so it seemed that no-one was interested in her now.

I left her out just a few nights more, but November was beginning. What would be the best place in the house for her? My study was the only real possibility. All the rooms in our house are a comfortable size, so even with a couple of bookcases, and my large desk for the computer there was still quite a bit of floor space. Importantly none of the other cats passed much time there now, so I decided that was where Sooty would spend her nights.

I wondered how Sooty would take to being brought into the house. I decided to put her in the cat basket and bring her in that way, just in case she struggled and I lost my hold on her. What was her reaction to coming into the house? She simply purred as if to say, "This is what I was hoping you would do."

During that November her appetite was phenomenal, confirming my conviction that she had been homeless for some while. At first the routine was that I brought her into the house well before dark and then put her outside at the bottom of the garden for some of the daytime. I took her off the Cats' Protection waiting list and decided I would find her a home. After all, we had never intended to have even five cats and I doubted whether Sooty could be integrated into my unwelcoming feline band. By the end of November I had her fully vaccinated and her age was estimated at around ten years old. Her behaviour showed that she clearly had nothing to learn about being a pet cat. She knew all about cat flaps and litter trays, and what is more, she had a firm conviction that there should be something nice for pussies coming out of the fridge. .

A friend, who had cared well for her previous cat into old age, expressed interest in her. If Sooty went there she would be in the house when Pat was home, but out in the garden while she was at work, but with access to a shed and cat bed. It was because a home there was a distinct possibility that I still put her out in the daytime. But Pat wanted a couple of weeks to think it over.

As I got to know Sooty I soon became very fond of her. In my prayers I found myself telling God that I would love to keep her and asking Him to work out what He wanted. But with the offer I had made, the outcome must depend on my friend's decision. Two weeks passed with no phone call so clearly it was not the case that Pat could not wait to take Sooty on. Then one day I plucked up courage to pick up the phone. What was her decision?

"I have decided this isn't the right time to take on a cat!" was the reply.

I did manage not to shout, "Hallelujah!" down the phone and I hope I sounded very understanding. I felt ecstatic!

Peter was more than happy for us to keep Sooty. She could now choose whether or not to go out in the daytime. Sooty chose! She had seen enough of the Great Outdoors, thank you! Now that she was in she simply was not going out. For the next few months, with maybe two brief exceptions, that was that. (After all, what are cat loos for?)

Confined to my study at night, she still chose to spend most of the day there. Just sometimes she would venture down into the living room and jump onto the broad back of the settee which is a safe place to snooze. It is also a good vantage point from which to keep an eye on the activities of other felines. On her first Christmas with us she delighted us all when she chose to come downstairs into the living room for most of the day, not perturbed by the presence of a very well-behaved dog belonging to one of our guests. She began her friendship with one other guest by sitting on her lap much of the time.

But she might have missed her first Christmas with us. I had provided everything I thought she needed in my study including a scratching post. The thick rope wound round this was beginning to come undone, but as it was thicker than my fingers I had not seen it as a hazard. One day when we were sitting downstairs I heard a banging upstairs and rushed to see what was wrong. Somehow Sooty had got tied up with this rope and got it also tied tightly round the leg of my desk In her panic to free herself she was threshing about, half strangling her middle and making matters a great deal worse.

I manipulated Sooty and the rope round the desk leg so as to get enough slack to untie it. She was petrified, but had suffered no harm. When I had freed her, I held her close to me for about twenty minutes or more until she calmed down. The cat scratcher went by the shortest route to the dustbin. I do try to keep an eye on everything in house and garden from the Feline Safety point of view, but here I had obviously failed badly and am so thankful to God that I found Sooty in time.

The other cats responded to Sooty's inclusion in the household with varying degrees of tolerance or hostility! Twinkle and Sooty, who are both very small cats, spent some time chasing each other round the house, probably to decide which was boss. Teazle generally did not think including Sooty was a good idea and even Lulu's behaviour towards her showed that she also disapproved. Tommy Primrose, my one-eyed monster, definitely took a dislike to her. Tigger's initial reaction was the most surprising: he was scared. Never mind the fact that he is at least twice her size. Cuddly and loveable, he may be, but he never was a hero. Our dear Tigger needed quite a lot of extra love and reassurance.

Sooty slotted herself into the middle of this lot with the minimum of fuss and trouble. As far as I could make out she did not approve of other cats anyway!

I remember one occasion when Tommy Primrose bonked her one on the head and in response her little paw went like a piston and she gave him six of the best in return, so rapidly that I think even he was taken by surprise. She soon learnt that if Tommy's attention was not focused on her, she could usually nip past him to a safe place before he could catch her, even when he found it worth launching himself into action. Sooty and Twinkle did share my lap on a few occasions, but I think that was because neither was prepared to give way to the other. Either of these two will spend hours there whenever they get the chance.

Sooty has developed her own routines. With the spring weather she began to explore the garden again and the later on she found herself quiet private places amongst the shady plants for a snooze on hot summer days. Come the winter and she practically gave up on the outside world again. Otherwise she remains either in my study, or on the back of the settee, a new kind of headrest for me! She is so much part of that settee that after sitting in the same room with her there for several hours, Peter asked, "Where's Sooty?"

Concentration on their weekly treat

Chapter 13: Six Cats in One Garden!

We live in a three bedroomed semi-detached house built in the nineteen thirties. There is something over a hundred feet of garden at the back in the usual rectangular shape one finds in town. About two thirds of this is ornamental and is divided by a rustic arch from the bottom of the garden where I try to squeeze fruit and vegetables out of a rather small area. That really is an attempt to get a quart out of a pint pot. As I have already mentioned, gardening is my main hobby. My six beloved pussies, that is six out of the last seven you have read about, have the potential to be my main garden pests! So how do we manage?

First of all I have deliberately decided that cats must be treated as more important than plants. After all, they are higher in the order of creation. There can be no doubt that cats have a whole range of feelings

which plants simply cannot have. It helps too to decide in advance that a damaged plant is not worth getting upset over.

The three females, Lulu, Twinkle and Sooty want to be exempted from my classification as garden pests. Lulu almost always uses a litter tray by day or by night. Twinkle and Sooty normally do their digging in secluded areas among the leaf litter and mulch under the shrubs, so that does not harm anything. So that shifts all the blame and responsibility on to the three toms, Tigger, Teazle and Tommy Primrose.

As I said earlier, Teazle is very territorial. I do not think he ever digs a hole to spend a penny since by the time he has sprayed everything he wants to spray, there cannot be enough left to make digging worth while! So I live with the result that here and there a shrub will have a dead branch low down, and a conifer a brown patch. He has killed one or two plants outright, but not too many. There are places in the garden where, if one gets too close, it is clear that the aroma assaulting the nose is not the perfume of flowers!

One cat has decided that the compost heap is the ideal cat loo and I could not agree more. What a pity Tommy Primrose does not come to the same conclusion! He is my most enthusiastic digger.

The ornamental section of the garden is thickly planted with shrubs, perennials and bulbs, so there is not much loose earth here. This, however, does not deter Tommy from excavations in this area. If I see him spending one of his half pint pennies amidst my plants I simply add half a gallon or so of water to it after he has moved away. Diluted like that it will not scorch the roots of my plants. It might even do them good.

The vegetable section with its more constant cultivation is much more tempting. After every planting, or seed sowing, I simply have to work out how to keep the cats off this particular area. A built in bonus is that most of what works for the cats will almost certainly work for the wood pigeons also. One ploy is to fix wire mesh over the soil. Another is to insert numerous sticks, even old raspberry canes cut up will do, so closely that the cats will not bother to walk on that patch. I did not meet with much success when I used horticultural fleece, as that, apparently, is a desirable cat bed and the carrots did not enjoy being incubated!

It is, of course, my responsibility to see that there is always somewhere left in my garden which will invite my cats to dig in it rather than go over the fence to someone else's patch! I cannot guarantee this works, but I must at least try. So a few days ago when I spread 'Silent Roar' over the cabbage seedlings, the runner beans which were just germinating and the newly sown carrots, I also raked over a patch of fine soil under the Bramley in the hope that will meet with feline approval. Tommy Primrose did approve.

'Silent Roar', which is made from lion's dung, is designed specifically to keep cats off the particular area of garden where it is spread. The idea is that they will think that a truly big cat has been there! The very next day Teazle was lying contently on the area over which I had spread the 'Silent Roar'. I guess it may well work with the majority of cats, but you always get the one who does not conform. So it was back to closely spaced sticks.

Lulu has her share of the treat in private

Certain plants make great places for cats to snooze. Somehow I get the feeling that the pale mauve form of Campanula glomerata would look better if Lulu had not had a morning nap in its middle! There will also be feline pathways in places convenient to those who use them and one might just as well accept that. Ornamental grasses will be chewed. If they make a tempting tuft, they may be pounced on, fought and scuffed! There was the occasion when Sparkle, as a youngster, charged full pelt over the rock garden and knocked off the only flower ever produced by Iris Winogradowii. I had paid four or five pounds for that bulb.

I often use a little plastic kneeler when I weed the garden. If I get up, I find I will have lost it to one of the cats. Peter and I put out our garden chairs and in no time Tigger and Teazle will occupy them. Tigger, of course, gives his delightful little grizzle when we remove him.

But when I go out into the garden the three toms usually follow me and trot around with me for a while. I do so enjoy this. One of them will solemnly walk down the path, while I have to go slow at his pace. When I fill a can with water, Tommy will begin to drink from it. On one occasion, just as he finished, I reflected, "That was tomorite!", but he was none the worse for this though I have been more watchful since.

Surely three heavyweight tom cats should see off any rats brazen enough to venture onto their patch? Well, so I thought for a long time. Then one day I met Tigger just by the bird table. Near him, looking as if they had not been properly introduced, was a half grown rat. It was unhurt, making no attempt to run away and Tigger was making no attempt to catch it.

The rat toddled off into the garden amongst the shrubs, followed, not only by Tigger, but by Tommy and Teazle as well. A total of about forty pounds of tom cat should be able to deal with one rat, not a big one at that. So I left them to it and went indoors. Twenty minutes later I went down the garden again. From amongst the shrubs emerged first the rat and then Teazle who was following it at a respectful distance. The rat walked round the edge of the pond, rather carelessly, as it fell in and then had to extract itself. Teazle kept his distance. The rat waddled off down by the fence and eventually disappeared under it, totally unharmed. The cats had done no more than politely escort it round the garden. This was so unlike the farm cats I grew up with. I think they had a better deal than a great many farm cats, as I never remember one of them not being in good condition, but they were expected to dispose of vermin.

This garden is not just for growing plants. It is the cats' core territory. I intend it should be a good place for them and also for hedgehogs and birds. I was brought up to enjoy creepy crawlies, those things with six or more legs! The two ponds we dug out ourselves are teeming with frogs, newts and great water beetles. Often the most interesting thing I see out there is not one of my plants. For example there has been the delight of watching a bright yellow ladybird hatch from its pupal stage and gradually darken to the orange with black spots with which we are all familiar. I have watched a newt delicately placing her eggs one by one on the pondweed. It was with some astonishment that Peter and I saw the frogs in the pond catch and eat the wasps which alighted on the weed there intending to have a drink.

When Sparkle was young the kindest thing I could do for the birds was scare them away before letting him out of doors! But now our present six cats, all aged between twelve and fourteen are less speedy. They seem to have changed from being hunters to becoming ornithologists. Indeed, they do spend a considerable time bird-watching, and it does the birds no harm! Our two pairs of resident blackbirds have sized them up accurately enough and know just the right distance to leave between themselves and the pussies.

Twinkle and Tommy Primrose having a siesta

Once spring growth has begun there are numerous nooks and crannies in the garden where the cats can rest in sun or shade, where even Lulu can feel safe from those tabbies. What they do love is for me to buy a bale of straw. When I give the minarette, (columnar) fruit trees a mulch of straw, it is worth making it extra thick, then it makes a choice cat bed for fine days and almost always there will be one or the other of the toms sprawled out on it. A part bale left anywhere will be used constantly for a feline siesta.

I put an old carpet on the compost heap to keep the heat in and that was one of the most popular things I ever did from the pussy point of view. After all, they had a slightly heated bed then! The compost heap catches the late sun and Teazle in particular spends his evenings on it until I fetch him indoors. In the cold greenhouse there are three bits of old carpet which take a little of my space on the greenhouse bench, but then pussies will sleep there and leave the rest for me. I have since put a woolly square over each piece of carpet there and this has boosted the popularity of these areas. I want to see that everything in the garden is safe for the cats, and for the other creatures who share it.

On a wet morning I do have rather a houseful of bored cats. They will go through into the greenhouse and peer out. The toms will venture out for a bit, come back and then I have wet cats wrapping themselves round my legs.

As I type Sooty snoozes on my lap. When I go downstairs and relax in the living room, any of the cats apart from Tommy Primrose might see this as the opportunity for a cuddle on my lap. Tommy will not be far away from his humans either. Sometimes I stop to wonder how these creatures, so very different from ourselves, can settle in and share our lives in a way which brings so much pleasure to both.

Our six cats are certainly all in the senior bracket, but then so are we: we have been Senior Citizens for some years. What does the future hold? If any of these cats, or their successors, outlive us, then they have a secure future with the Cinnamon Trust. For Peter and myself, we do know God holds the future and that He is to be trusted.

I'm holding Tigger

Born in 1935 Audrey Nash, nee Barcock, grew up on a nursery garden-cum-poultry farm in Suffolk with plenty of four-footed friends, which always included cats. Having read English and later Theology, she taught in secondary schools for fifteen years.

She then married Peter, a Baptist minister, and left teaching to support him in his ministry. Initially they had just the cat Audrey owned at the time of their marriage, but later on cats were either passed on to them, or arrived of their own accord, so that they ended up with six at once.

They are now enjoying their retirement along with some of the senior pussies you can read about in this book.

Printed in the United Kingdom by
Lightning Source UK Ltd., Milton Keynes
138921UK00001B/267/P